Children, Structure, and Agency

Routledge Studies in Development and Society

Children, Structure, and Agency

Realities Across the Developing World

G.K. Lieten

Routledge
Taylor & Francis Group
New York   London

First published 2008
by Routledge
711 Third Avenue, New York, NY 10017

Simultaneously published in the UK
by Routledge
2 Park Square, Milton Park, Abingdon, Oxon OX14 4RN

Routledge is an imprint of the Taylor & Francis Group, an informa business

First issued in paperback 2012

© 2008 Taylor & Francis

Typeset in Sabon by IBT Global.

Library of Congress Cataloging-in-Publication Data

Lieten, Georges Kristoffel, 1946–
    Children, structure and agency : realities across the developing world / by G.K. Lieten.
        p. cm. — (Routledge studies in development and society ; 16)
    Includes bibliographical references and index.
    ISBN 978-0-415-98973-2
    1. Child welfare—Cross-cultural studies.   2. Children—Services for—Cross-cultural studies.   I. Title.
    HV713.L545 2008
    362.709172'4—dc22   2007050577

ISBN13: 978-0-415-98973-2 (hbk)
ISBN13: 978-0-415-53665-3 (pbk)
ISBN13: 978-0-203-89526-9 (ebk)

Contents

List of Tables and Boxes

TABLES

BOXES

Glossary

BJP	Bharatya Janata Party, a right-wing Hindu party in India
Chamar	One of the lowest castes in India, traditionally involved in leather craft
Chappati	Flat round bread
Chhach	Curd mixed with water
Chulha	Small freestanding oven
Chungse	Vietnamese word akin to agency
Churma	Flour fried with *ghee* and sweetened with sugar
Dal	Lentils, a staple food in India
Doi moi	Economic modernisation and liberalisation in Vietnam
Dong	Vietnamese currency
Favela	Slum area in Latin America
Feman	Relief work
Garibi hatao	A program under Indira Gandhi to put an end to poverty
GDP	Gross Domestic Product
Khaini	Chewing tobacco
Kichri	Cooked rice with *dal*
Kutcha	Solid
Lifafa	Envelope
Lungi	A cloth worn by males in India, wrapped around the lower part of the body
Machista	Male (chauvinist) behaviour, a stereotype ascription for Latin American males
Masaala	A mixture of (usually hot) spices
NGO	Nongovernmental organisation

Prasad	Offering in the temple
Roti	Flat rounded bread, similar to *chappati*
Subji	Vegetables
Toli	Ward, living quarters
Ujaama	Tanzania political system under Nyerere, development based on villages and community
UNDP	United Nations Development Programme
Voceador	The bus attendant (Latin America) shouting the bus direction and attracting passengers

Preface

This book reflects the findings of a study conducted in six countries (Vietnam, India, Burkina Faso, Tanzania, Bolivia, and Nicaragua) on the issue of child participation in development.

The perception of the child as a self-conscious actor and as a bearer of rights is relatively new. According to the view underlying the pedagogy of liberation, which witnessed a short upsurge in the Western countries in the 1970s, children themselves are seen as causative agents. Children have rights. The need for care, access to education and health services are some of the rights high on their priority list. They also like to be respected and to be valued for what they are and what they think. By empowering children to make people listen to them, children can play a more active role in their community. Such a view combines, but also contrasts with the more traditional view of the child as the recipient of knowledge and the recipient of rights.

There is a need to explore this field and gain better insight in the potential of children under different circumstances. The research program has been sponsored by PLAN International in the Netherlands. Being a child-focused development organisation, the organisation is devoted to realising lasting improvements in the quality of life of deprived children all over the world. Like other organisations focussing on children, it places children in the centre of development processes and takes the Child Rights Convention as the guiding principle. It is unusual for NGOs to financially support research which goes beyond the mere stage of monitoring and assessment of projects. PLAN's involvement in the program is really exceptional. By doing so the organisation has shown vision and courage. I hope the results are appropriate to the expectation and that some of the issues that have been raised can lead to policy formulations.

The research was conducted by the Amsterdam-based foundation for International Research on the Exploitation of Working Children (IREWOC). IREWOC was established in 1991 in order to generate more research on child labour, and to raise awareness and motivate action around this complex issue. In order to monitor and understand child labour situations, it is necessary to look at the wider context of the living conditions of children and their families.

Many people have contributed to this book. The project was conducted in six countries and the chief investigators in those countries, together with their team, have done an exceptionally good job in providing the material and publishing studies on their own countries: Le Thi Quy in Vietnam; Anoop Satpathy, Anup Karen, and Piush Anthony in India; Miranda van Reeuwijk, Daniel Ngemera, and LeAnne Fries in Tanzania; Omer Ibrahim Omer in Burkina Faso; David Layme Llamos, Edgar Moreno Valdivia, and Marten van den Berge in Bolivia; and Luis Hector Serra and Marcia Castillo Sequeria in Nicaragua. In all these countries we have profited from the logistic and mental support of the PLAN staff. Marten van den Berge, Afke De Groot, Albertine de Lange, Godefroid Nimbona, and Heike Roschanski of the IREWOC bureau in Amsterdam have helped me in developing my ideas for this book and Sonja Zweegers has done an excellent job in editing and clarifying the manuscript. I am greatly indebted to all of them.

The focus in this book is on the situation of children living in adverse conditions. The perception of the working child itself is of increasing interest in the discussion on street children, child labour, and children in unfavourable circumstances in general. Research needs to be undertaken on the social and cultural parameters of child labour and particularly on how the child conceives the work, the role in the family context, the (missed opportunities of) education, and the challenges of the future. That is the first step in participation and the first step in agency: adults listening to what the children have to say. I hope that this book contributes to that aim.

Kristoffel Lieten, Amsterdam, August 2007

Introduction

One of the new departures in recent research, partially related to interest in child labour and in universal literacy as a Millennium Development Goal, has been the growing attention to children and the discovery of both 'children' and 'childhood' as research areas. Children have become visible in ways that they were not before. The policy concerns relate to the inclusion of children in the development process, the abuse and deprivation of children, and the contextualisation of the rights associated with 'childhood'. In the mainstream construction of childhood, children are now seen as individuals with an autonomy that should be safeguarded and fostered. That contention will be a constant concern throughout this book. The debate on childhood and on the rights of children in fact is also a discussion on the implication of various dichotomies: individualism and the common good, self-assertion and protection, claims and duties, rights and needs, and the needy and the affluent.

Close encounters with children, particularly when eliciting their voices and learning how they live their lives, add a new dimension on how the world of the big and adult should deal with the world of the small and young. Many of the books on child rights have been written from a Western position and with empirical data from the affluent Western world of childhood (Zelizer 1985; Corsaro 1997; James and Prout 1997; James, Jenks, and Prout 1998; Qvortrup 1994, 2005). Detailed fieldwork in developing countries allows for a realistic assessment of how the lives and values of children in those regions of the world are structured. The findings may indicate variations between different societies and yet simultaneously also have cross-cultural similarities.

In the acceptance of the universal principles underlying the Child Rights Convention (CRC) of 1989, a singular standard notion of childhood, and the rights associated with it, was decreed as official policy. The imposition (and official acceptance) of such a universal norm has not gone uncontested. A number of scholars and NGOs suppose that culture and context in many (developing) countries are so dissimilar that a universal norm of childhood is in fact an imposition of alien (Western) norms.

This book discusses this dilemma. Is it proper to speak of one standard of childhood, or does a universal definition impose Western dominance on other cultures? Do non-Western cultures have traditionally established types of childhood that need to be protected against the universalising tendencies of institutions and initiatives such as the UN (the CRC) and the ILO (articles 138 and 182 against child labour)?

This book studies the lives of children in six developing countries against the background of development, modernisation, and globalisation. These phenomena are severely value laden, often equated with Coca-Cola, McDonald's, Christian values, Hollywood and pop music. There definitely are other aspects of development, modernisation, and globalisation which are less contested—for example, the introduction of universal elementary education and gender equality. This book explores how children manage to appreciate these aspects and how they deal with them in their daily lives.

The emphasis on the dominant local culture, and the locally constructed childhood, which many scholars tend to prefer, tends to ignore the various economic, cultural, and social attributes of a modernising and globalising world. If globalisation has a meaning, then it is that people all over the world, even in the communities that hitherto have maintained their traditional lifestyles, are confronted with outside influences. Such influences may have multiplied and intensified, but they have always been at work throughout the history of the world as Wolf (1982) has so splendidly documented in his classic book with a sarcastic title, *Europe and the People Without History*. The external influences compel people to adjust their economic, social, and cultural patterns. Changes that are adopted in a community under the impact of internal dynamism and external influence are assimilated by the children. They impact the way in which all children are raised in their particular environments, whether poor or rich, boy or girl.

In the villages across the developing world, there are few settings in which children do not participate actively. Children are active in daily routine tasks within the family; parents socialise the children into managing the resources that guarantee their livelihoods, such as livestock and land. The daily activities help the children to develop skills, attain knowledge, formulate attitudes, and build social networks. In such practices, children show and demonstrate that they have a potential for agency and that they can play an effective role within their families and communities.

The perception of the child as a self-conscious actor and as a bearer of rights is relatively new, but, as Purdy (1992, 87–123) has shown, many experiments, in line with the philosopher Rousseau's childrearing theory, have been put in place, allowing children to develop autonomously, as liberated individuals. She concludes that if children have equal rights and can fully participate in the planning of their own lives and environment, they are less likely to develop enabling virtues such as self-discipline, thoughtfulness, and a moral understanding of right and wrong. The antiauthoritarian pedagogy, which had some following in the Western world in the 1970s, also went a long way in liberating children from parental dominance. Purdy

(1992, 55) has made the following sobering observation: 'it requires that the child make judgments about interests, not just seek immediate gratification and avoidance of pain. To make judgments about interests and act upon them, children must know a good deal about how the world and other people operate, and they must possess substantial self-control'.

Yet, the idea of children as liberated participants quickly has come to occupy a central place in many child-centred approaches and quite a number of international child-focussed aid agencies actually take such an approach as the foundation for their work. The assumption is that if children were allowed to develop of their own accord and act as agents of change, they would produce a better society. Children are presumed to be flexible agents and to actually have a right to be as free and participative as adults. In the entire range of articles in the CRC, the focus tends to rest on child participation. Childhood is considered not as a stage in which a child has to be protected from impairing forces and has to be guided into maturity, but as a stage of full entitlements. The autonomy of the child rather than its immaturity is taken as the principle for intervention. Such an approach, relying more on their innate potential for action and planning, takes children as young adults. The most outspoken child liberation advocates assert that no agewise distinctions are justifiable and that childhood actually is adulthood. Childhood, Liebel (2004, 7) argues, 'is regarded not as a special sphere in which as yet immature and undeveloped creatures have to be protected and promoted, but as a sphere in which children too count as people of equal value, having the right and the ability to be supported, to have their say, and to take part in decisions as and when they wish to begin working'.

The agency approach, like the interactionist approach, tends to take the child as a unified category. While stressing participation, agency, and autonomy, one should not lose sight of the position of the family within the economic system, the social support system and the cultural norms that affect the environment and the very competencies of the children. To the extent that children are social actors, they find themselves, like adults, in an environment shaped by their circumstances. The social and economic structure, and the location of the child's family within that structure, determines the parameters of childhood and the parameters of agency. There is no such thing as a free-floating 'agent'. The focus on the exemplary child, the child which fits the role model of the participative and knowledgeable child, tends to neglect the socioeconomic aspects in which the child is embedded and which may prevent many children from imbibing that role model:

> This could imply that the initial ethical standpoint, wishing to give a voice to children, is at risk, since the new pedagogy of participation may very well be silencing specific groups of children and their parents. . . . We argue that the dichotomist thinking on power relations between

children and adults, masks forms of exclusion *among* children and adults, as both may be embedded in regimes of truth that favour white, middle-class educational practices. (Vandenbroeck and Bouverne 2006, 128 and 130).

An understanding of how children deal with their circumstances therefore requires studies, which include specific groups of children, who did not have a voice, neither in the old protective approach nor in the new participative approach. Close reading is needed with a focus on the daily lives of children, their cognitive understanding and emotional reactions, their interactions with each other and with adults of various kinds, and their strategies of action. That is the intent of this book. The main aim of the study was to investigate the daily lives of children in poverty-stricken societies and to examine in what sense children are actively exerting agency and participating in the development of their communities.

1 Tradition and Child-Centred Approaches

All communities have social practices into which its members are inducted from an early age onwards; this is referred to as the process of primary socialisation, with gender-sensitive and age-defined roles and rituals. In the past, local communities used to be relatively stable and individual roles and functions were acquired through the imitation of the existing norms and practices. The individual was expected to act socially. The participation of the child meant that it adhered to the tradition and to the changes therein. Submission to hierarchy was paramount.

Most parents themselves, in hierarchically organised and autocratic societies, may never have been exposed to the ideas of rights and participation. Caste-ridden, tribal, and orthodox religious communities are usually organised, with the notable exceptions, around the authority of specified elders who see to it that tradition is observed. Growing up in a rural environment usually happens far away from the modernising impact of cities and hardly touched by the expanding opportunities of economic development. Ideas and models of a different behaviour or alternative choices, which could provide the impetus to pro-change activities from below, are often missing.

On the other hand, communities rather always have been changing. The unchanging idea of tradition often is a stereotype, imposed from the outside in order to essentialise local cultures as the Other. The use of those cultural stereotypes has often followed a static and homogenising view; cultures are seen as applying to all members of the community. The emphasis on dichotomies between developed and underdeveloped societies rather than on similarities across ethnic groups is the bottom line of such an approach.

The logic of such an approach implies that there are no universal values and norms, and that 'Western ethnocentricity' is at play if such norms are assumed to be applicable throughout the world. This assertion that the Western world is imposing its norms on developing countries has become prominent in some of the postmodernist literature of recent years; it has allowed scholars to argue that child labour is not necessarily repugnant, but that it is actually embedded in local cultures, and should thus be respected.

In the discussion on the concept of *childhood*, some have embraced the notion that a childhood involving protection and emotional care is typical only for Western cultures. This perspective takes as its starting point the assertion that children have rights not so much to protection as to participation and even to work. In developing countries, work is presumed to be part and parcel of the everyday existence of most children (Liebel et al. 2001; Liebel 2004; Cussianovich 2002, 2; James et al. 1998, 107 and 112). Jo Boyden (1997, 208), for example, has argued that taking Western childhood as a normative basis for remedial action elsewhere could potentially have damaging effects on poor families and their children. She postulates that the beliefs of 'welfare and rights practitioners' differ radically from those of parents and children. The former consider children who are absent from school, children at work or living in the streets, as aberrations that need to be rectified. The parents, Boyden adds, may not conceive it as a problem and may consider work as an integral part of normal socialisation: 'In this respect, the move to set global standards for childhood and common policies for child welfare may be far from the enlightened steps anticipated by its proponents'.

The argument against imposing universal norms partially derives from the assumption that childhood is a pluriform concept and that the 'Western' idea of childhood should not find universal application. The work by Philippe Ariès (1964) is usually taken as the standard reference work. What Ariès has done is to show, on the basis of visual representations, that family life, which was formally a peculiarity only of the aristocracy and the bourgeoisie, progressively extended into the entire society in the course of the eighteenth century. From the eighteenth century onwards, the family started to form as a separate and private reality, and the child acquired a different character: the parents are preoccupied with its education, its capacity building, its future (Ariès 1964, 457). This evolution was, for a long time, restricted to 'the nobility, the bourgeoisie, the rich artisans, the rich workers', and in the nineteenth century even 'a big chunk of the population, the poorest and most numerous, lived as the medieval families, the children not staying with their parents' (1964, 457).

The historical evolution in Europe thus suggests that the emergence of a new type of family, with a new type of childhood, was not culture specific. It was class specific and emerged and fructified in the midst of wider economic changes (towards modernity). Families in the developing countries today, possibly with the exception of tiny groups living on the margins, in areas that are geographically difficult to access, have made that transition from the 'collective' to the private: children are looked after within the households with the future of the individuals in mind.

The process of long-term historical evolution has led to new forms of socialisation; forms which emerged and which gradually entered mainstream society. Under the impact of development, modernisation, commoditisation, and spatial integration, changes in ideas, norms, and attitudes have come along and the socialisation process of children has thus become embedded in those new normative parameters. The process has become ingrained in the 'private family', rather than the community, as the nodal point of child welfare and education. It has also become entrenched in an economic environment where survival is a matter of acquiring the best competitive endowments in an expanding world. (See e.g., Katz 2004 on children in Sudan under the impact of globalisation.) The endowments relate to a proper education, good health, and access to the wider world. That apparently is what childhood is about, both in the developed world and in the developing world.

QUESTIONS OF CHILDHOOD: UNIVERSALISM AND INDIVIDUALISM

Breaking down childhood as a concept would help to distil the pan-cultural from the specific Western features underlying the concept (Fernando 2001, 20). In the debate on 'childhood', many authors have argued that childhood is a social construct.[1] Their paradigm is that 'Western' childhood is only one of the multiple constructs and that this construct should not be imposed as a general standard on all the children in the world. The various authors who defend the idea of multiple concepts of childhood are keen to stress that children should be understood within their own world order and without the imposition of the universal normative model. They thus appear to take an anticolonial stance, liberating childhood from the Western and colonising narrative. The CRC, they argue, has reinforced 'Western' norms under the garb of universalism. White (1999, 134), for example, argues that the official policies are 'often based on static and universalising models of childhood', and prefers to take the middle ground, resorting to cultural relativism as a tool of learning and understanding. Cultural relativism 'in addition to the general principle of respect for the ways of life of others (is) a useful corrective to pseudo-universalistic notions' (White 1999, 137).

The universal objectives and values of the CRC have been characterised, by a number of scholars, as being derived from Western values and Western lifestyles. William Myers (1999) sees in the CRC an excessive orientation towards the values of the North and West, 'with too little recognition of values from other regions of the world', and argues that despite the universal ratification, it has an 'unmistakable rich country flavour, as well as a whiff of paternalism in which the powerful rich dictate how the poor should raise their children'. He also draws our attention to the fact that

---

1. For example: Philippe Ariès 1964; Neil Postman 1984; Zelizer 1985; Stephen 1995; James and Prout 1997; Corsaro 1997; White 1999; Nieuwenhuys 1998; Miljeteig 2000; Liebel 2004; Qvortrup 2005b.

'the Convention incorporates a highly individualistic view of children and child development that typifies industrialised countries but does not accord with the majority of the world's cultures, who tend to understand children as an integral part of the family and society, and as having responsibilities as well as rights'.

Some child-centred development aid organisations, possibly in their endeavour to be closer to the 'community', have taken aspects of that discourse on board, defending local cultures in their construction of childhood. The International Save the Children Alliance (2000), for example, has commented on childhood in the following antiuniversalistic manner: 'There is no standard or universal way of being a child or of being in the state of childhood'. The state of being a child and the concept of childhood as a particular period in the human life cycle, the document states, can vary greatly from one society and culture to another:

> Despite universal biological processes determining children's maturation and development, there are also considerable differences in societies' and cultures' interpretations of these processes and in the ways in which social practices interact with biological processes to produce specific individual and cultural capabilities and identities. There are probably as many versions of childhood as there are children in the world, since children—like adults—are persons with individual experiences, ideas and capabilities despite the demands of our various cultures.

The theorem of childhood as a social construct has, in the above citation, developed further into childhood as a cultural construct and even as an individual construct ('as many versions of childhood as there are children'), and as such reveals that the notion of childhood has become subject to cultural relativism. It is assumed that cultures, whatever a 'culture' means, are different all over the world and that all cultures have an innate right to autonomy and equivalence with other cultures.

If childhood is a social construct, what does it mean? Is it a concept that is used as an analytical category in order to delineate a social phenomenon, in which case childhood need not have different meanings for different societies? Or is it a concept which has different meanings in different societies, in which case societies, diachronically and synchronically, have different childhoods? Qvortrup (2005a, 2) makes a reference to Ariès according to whom in the medieval and immediate postmedieval period children in Europe did not constitute a conceptual category. They were not perceived as a separate category with distinct needs and they were fully participating in adult society, in its work, its leisure, its public events: 'the Arièsian vision was one in which children were a part of *public* life . . . and to be in the open space implied visibility, albeit not in the figure of children as a group or collectivity.' The emergence of childhood meant that children started to live in a social sphere (the family, the school) that was separate from the world of adults and that took the distinct needs and capacity of the child into consideration. Qvortrup (2005a, 4) further suggests that the position of children, and the attitudes of adults towards children, was altered by the changes in the mode of production as a consequence of which the usefulness of children as direct producers declined and their usefulness as future producers, properly skilled, increased. It thus appears, at least in this interpretation, that childhood is a separate stage in life, the absence of which, for example in the case of severely exploitative child labour, would lead to a 'lost childhood' or a 'stolen childhood'.

If the meaning of childhood is the stage distinguishing them from adults, then would there be scope for a variety of childhoods (or a variety of adult-hoods) and the illegitimacy of imposing a universal norm of child rights (or a universal norm of human rights)? Children across the globe live different lives and the argument for a plurality of childhoods 'has often been related to the global disparity between affluent and poor countries and regions, as well as to class divisions, variation between cultures and differences between cohorts' (Frones 2005, 268). In this reading, the variety of childhoods is linked to the variety of children's lives as social practice. In the sense of social practice there possibly are as many childhoods as there are children, but using such a connotation would make the concept analytically hollow. Children move along starkly different paths. Childhood, says Frones, is something which children *do*, and what they do can show marked differences, not only across cultures but also across class positions, age, and gender: 'The synchronic patterns allow a variety of positions at each phase, a variety that is increasing with the differentiation of modern society, producing a correspondingly large number of possible diachronic tracks and paths' (2005, 275). This actually is the paradox of the homogenisation of childhood within child-centred institutions and the differentiation in the actual world of children.

It is important to make that distinction between childhood as an analytical category, referring to the basic principles underlying the position of the child in society, and childhood as living practice: '*Being* a child is defined as belonging within the framework of childhood. The lives of children as *social practice* are represented by the processes of moving through childhood' (Frones 2005, 281). That distinction is usually not made and leads many, including some child aid organisations, as the quote above illustrates, to the conclusion that children in developing countries have a different childhood and, moreover, that a Western ideal-type childhood should not be imposed on them.

The discussion on childhood, and the turn against universalism, carving out the legitimacy of a separate childhood for children in developing countries, misses the concrete point of the social relations and the institutional structures that a child is embedded in. Childhood in a squalid urban neighbourhood in Western countries may not be that different from the childhood experience and constraints in a poor neighbourhood in cities of the

Third World. What is missing in the concept of childhood is the concrete analysis of how poor and/or ethnically marginalised children are made to remain in a state of childhood that, although institutions such as the educational system formally have become equivalent, puts them in a disadvantageous position vis-à-vis the more fortunate children of the world. It is the social relations that provide some children in developing countries with a 'Western' childhood practice (school, leisure, music, sports, etc.) and others with a 'traditional' childhood practice (girls working in the kitchen and boys collecting garbage). A multitude of such distinctions within childhood also apply to children in distinctly different positions in the developed world. Defending the separate and specific childhood of deprived children then in fact would amount to defending, or at least condoning, their economic marginalisation. Children may remain bereft of a 'Western' type of childhood, not because of a different cultural perspective of childhood but because of the unfortunate impact of a globally lopsided economic development. In their case, universal ideals of childhood should not be abandoned for being alien or inappropriate (Rizzini and Dawes, 2001).

The discussion on childhood, separating a Western childhood from a non-Western childhood and warning against a one-sided imposition of universal values, does tend to overlook two important features.

The first feature is that of the globalising world in which ever larger territories and populations are absorbed into comparable historical circumstances. For children living in the *favelas* of Rio de Janeiro, the suburbs of Beijing, the villages of Bangladesh, the mountain slopes of the Himalayas, or the oases of the Sahara, it is less important what specific 'culture' they live in and how children used to live traditionally. Their concern now is that their future is determined by the struggle for livelihood in a 'modernising' world and that they have to acquire the enabling skills and knowledge. The process of socialisation at a local level has to keep the challenges and requirements of the new world, rather than those of the traditional culture, at the core of its attention.

The second feature is that traditional cultures are imbued with elements that are in conflict with what modern civil society seemingly represents: gender equality of boys and girls in their access to a secular education system and to a healthcare infrastructure that helps them battle death and disease. It seems fair to assume that these universal concerns should take precedence over traditional cultural rules, at least if we accept the implications of a globalising world. Unpacking the concept of childhood will without a doubt put some features apart as features of childhood that need to be universally respected. Moreover, these ideals are not alien, because the 'Western' childhood has been present in the families of the better-off sections of the developing world since colonial, and definitely since postcolonial times. After independence all the governments of these countries declared that universal education and a labour-free childhood of all the children should be an obligation of the state. It is important to remain aware of ethnocentric views, but also of the pitfalls of cultural relativism. Both these views may be academic constructs and adult-centric perceptions rather than a real reflection of what children themselves perceive as constituting their ideal childhood.

CHILD RIGHTS

A pan-cultural ideal of childhood has now become the norm in a globalising world. The 1989 Convention on the Rights of the Child (CRC) reinforced that norm. Despite the fact that too many nations do not live up to their own minimum standards—children still suffer from poverty, homelessness, abuse, neglect, preventable diseases, and unequal access to education—more countries have ratified the Convention than any other human rights treaty in history. Only the United States and Somalia have failed to ratify it. The near universal and rapid ratification of the Convention has given it a rare kind of legal and moral legitimacy.

When countries ratify the Convention, they agree to review their laws, social services, and funding relating to children. Governments are then obliged to take all necessary steps to ensure that the minimum standards set by the Convention in these areas are being met. The CRC refers to various protective measures, which could not possible be objectionable, particularly with regard to nutrition, clothing, and housing (Article 27), the right to the 'highest standard of health and medical care available' (Article 24), to 'free and compulsory education' (Article 28), and to protection 'from all forms of physical or mental violence, injury or abuse, neglect or negligent treatment, maltreatment or exploitation' (Article 19). It establishes clear norms and standards that the international community and state governments must comply with, and it is therefore a tool of social mobilisation:

- nondiscrimination (Article 2), which asserts that all children, regardless of their race, colour, gender, language, religion, opinion, disability, condition of birth, or any other characteristic, have the same right to develop their potential
- the right to survival and development (Article 6), which underscores the crucial need to ensure equity of opportunity and equitable access to basic social services
- the respect for the views of the children
- best interest of the child (Article 3), which stipulates that the child's best interest must be a 'primary consideration' in all actions concerning children

Many of these articles usually go uncontested, although of course a different meaning will be read in such a right as 'the best interest of the child'. More debatable are the clauses on participation. It is exactly these clauses that some international child-centred organisations, including UNICEF, have foregrounded as some of the more substantial child rights. The CRC indeed has often been used as the fountainhead of the idea of child participation. The specific novelty of the CRC is that it has transformed children from mere 'objects' of rights into active 'subjects' and 'holders' of rights. It does mention participation as a basic right of children, but it is also very cautious to stress the responsibilities, rights, and duties of the parents. Article 5 states that the parents shall provide, 'in a manner consistent with the evolving capacities of the child, appropriate direction and guidance in the exercise by the child of the rights recognized in the present Convention'. Article 12 says that children have the right to express their views in all matters affecting them, but this should not be construed to mean that children should now tell their parents what to do. The intent of the article is to encourage adults to listen to the children and involve them in decision-making—not, it seems, to give children authority over adults.

In promoting the right of expression, the CRC recognizes that such participation must occur in a manner that is appropriate to the child's level of maturity. It actually leaves the responsibility with the parents (and other adults who may have an interaction with the children, such as teachers and social welfare workers) to consider the child's views and use that information to make decisions that will be in the child's best interests. The CRC states:

> State Parties shall assure to the child who is capable of forming his or her own views the right to express those views freely in all matters affecting the child, the views of the child being given due weight in accordance with the age and maturity of the child (Article 12.1).

The rights contained in the Convention thus have to be handled by adults, depending on the age of the child, as stated earlier 'in a manner consistent with the evolving capacities of the child' (Article 5). Children, as the preamble to the Convention says, are prepared for a responsible adulthood where they shall live 'in the spirit of the ideals proclaimed in the Charter of the United Nations and in particular in the spirit of peace, dignity, tolerance, freedom, equality and solidarity'. The CRC thus could not possibly be used to argue that children have an unqualified right to participation, unless of course one assumes that children have an innate predisposition towards peace, tolerance, equality, and solidarity and that these values do not have to be inculcated and guarded. Moreover, Article 3, which guarantees 'the child's best interest', is usually seen as having priority over Article 12.

In the threesome *Provision, Protection, Participation*, the latter may always have to play third fiddle to the other two fundamental obligations that adults have vis-à-vis the child. Particularly in poverty-struck and child-inhospitable environments, provision and protection may outdistance participation as policy priorities. It in any case is a consideration to be discussed. There are various gradations of how participation should be applied, and how participation relates to other aims of intervention. Autonomous participation appears to represent the last of three meanings which Laderchi (2001, 4) has assigned to the concept: participation 'as a process *by* the people to whom development projects and programs are aimed, or *for* the people (with a development agency taking the initiative and often limiting participation to consultation) or *with* the people'. Substitute the child for people, we shall have the option between spending time and energy in creating an environment in which the children will develop by themselves or in which they will develop in a process guided by adults and within a socioeconomic environment which first has provided a relatively level field for all the children.

Let us further consider some of the complexities associated with 'participation'. As a concept, it is attractive and fits a long history of strategic thinking on development interventions. It is attractive since it makes the object of development into its own subject (the child as agent of development) and defends the promotion of a child-based (or people-based) path of development. As a concept, however, 'participation' is also elusive. Some concepts in their commonsense usage have a self-explanatory, self-regulatory, and self-legitimating ring to them. Looking at the precise meaning of the word, however, many different interpretations will be revealed. Some authors have looked at the various meanings which participation, for example, can have. Hart (1997, 41) has used a ladder as a metaphor to illustrate the different degrees of involvement children can have. The ladder shows the various forms in which adults (project holders) can involve the children. Some of these forms are regarded as mere tokenism or, even worse, manipulation.

One of the problems with this model is that it is highly abstract, isolated from social reality. What in one context indeed may amount to tokenism, in another context may signify a significant step towards visibility and involvement. Whereas Hart has developed his ladder exclusively for children, others have done a similar exercise for adults. Whereas Hart perceives participation in terms of information sharing and initiation of activities, Goetze (1994) has more abstract categories like passive participation, functional participation, and interactive participation and recommends self-mobilisation as the highest stage. The highest stage in Hart's typology is when children have developed so much competence and confidence that they can request the involvement of adults as experts, and that they do this from a position of power.

Another problem is the handing over of power. Is it the highest and ultimate aim of participation? How is power to be shared and delegated? One wonders about the implications and the procedures to be followed. If power is merely constituted by a majority vote, one would expect the children, the majority in any child-centred project, to have a free go at resources, structures, and plans. Such a position could be bad for the children, would be

Table 1.1 Typologies of (Child) Participation

Hart	Goetze	UNICEF	World Bank
Child-initiated, shared decisions with adults	Self-mobilisation	Analysing situations and making choices	
Child-initiated and directed		Initiating ideas, proposals and projects	Social invention
Adult-initiated, shared with children	Interactive participation	Being informed and consulted in decision making	Social learning
	Functional participation	Taking part in activities and processes	
	Participation by material incentives		
Consulted and informed	Participation by consultation	Forming views, expressing ideas	
Assigned but informed	Participation in information giving	Seeking information	Consulting
	Passive participation		Listening
Tokenism			
Decoration			External expert stance
Manipulation			

Sources: Hart (1997, also 1992), Goetze (1994), UNICEF (2003), World Bank (1996).

bad for the adults, would be bad for the community, and could be bad for all other provisions for protection and development.

Both approaches of Hart and Goetze, and the approach of UNICEF and the World Bank as well, appear to work within the framework of 'projects'. This is explicitly stated in the design of the World Bank, which also seems to have embraced the concept of participation wholeheartedly. Participation, according to the World Bank, is identified as: 'the process through which stakeholders influence and share control over development initiatives and the resources and decisions that affect them.' The argument is that projects hitherto usually have been designed and implemented by outsiders. A first step in the transition from the 'external expert stance' to the 'participatory stance' is to listen to the stakeholders and consult them at the various stages of project conception and implementation. This new participatory stance will take the experts inside the local social system and will require them to collaborate with the key stakeholders. Together, they conduct the analysis and decide what is needed and how it is to be achieved. In other words, they collaboratively set the objectives and create the strategy. It is a matter of overturning the direction of 'who learns what', a formulation which is akin to what Chambers (1983) stood for. The explanation why many projects failed, it is argued, is that there was insufficient 'social learning', i.e., stakeholders generating and internalising knowledge and attitudes.

In the child-participation paradigm, an identical role has been assigned to children. Many child-oriented programmes were said to have floundered because the children were not the driving force in projects. A project applying the new approach of social learning therefore should become 'child-initiated and child-directed'. The children as stakeholders, individually and collectively, will develop insights and understanding which will allow them to devise ways to obtain the objectives, which they themselves set. Such participation is meant 'to engage the poor', and the children of the poor, 'in their own development' in a bottom-up approach.

Children are then being promoted as mature and responsible subjects who have to come forward with their own insights and solutions. Some organisations, particularly Save the Children (Swift 1998; Woll 2000; Black 2004; Lansdown 2005), go to great extremes in according children a responsibility as agents of change or as agents for change in their own right, assuming that children know best what is good for them.

In one such participation exercise by Save the Children, children in Vietnam, Lesotho, Guyana, and Honduras were involved in the public consultation on the PRSPs. That participation, it was stated, was a right accruing to children but it would also improve official decision making. The following longish quote will illustrate how the organisation looks at the participation of children, which in this case is regarded as a step forward, but as not yet allowing the children to take the lead, which should be the ultimate aim:

> Children and young people provide a unique view of the impact of poverty on families. They often voice truths that adults no longer notice, or which socialised adults are wary of expressing, such as the link between poverty and family violence or substance abuse. Children's experiences are crucial in understanding how poverty affects families at household levels, including decisions about education and the allocation of scarce resources such as money or food. Children and young people's involvement in PRSPs can include: *contributing to policy dialogue* (doing research, providing information, expressing views, lobbying on the content), *contributing to implementation* (involvement in community-level implementation projects) and *monitoring* and *evaluation* (assessing whether budgets are getting through to local level, evaluating achievements). They can participate at *various levels*: in small-scale local community forums, by representation at

district or regional initiatives, and at national-level consultations or representation at meetings. The timescale of their involvement can vary from participation in one-off research consultations through to sustained participation over several years. Because of the technical nature of PRSPs, and the fact that children and young people's participation is only at a fledgling stage, most participatory initiatives have centred on large-scale consultations to gather views and experiences. This is a step forward, but it does not involve children and young people taking the lead in decision-making around the advocacy process. Nevertheless, these consultative initiatives are a good start. (O'Malley 2004, 1)

Agency has popped up as a new way of referring to this active involvement from below. Agency can be construed as self-determination, or free will; it is the power of individuals to act independently of the determining constraints of social structure. Agency presupposes a more active role of the target group and of the individual particularly. It starts from the assumption that the children targeted by the intervention are actually agents themselves, continuously acting in and reacting to circumstances. In fact, they should be allowed to be change agents in a dynamic process. The top-down process which looks after children and negates the dynamic process, it is argued by the participation advocates, fails to bring out the energy, imagination, and knowledge of the children.

The perception of the child as a self-conscious actor and as a bearer of rights developed in the 1970s, based partially on the theories of Piaget and partially on the general tendency to stress individual freedom and value. According to the view underlying the pedagogy of liberation, which then witnessed a short upsurge in the Western countries, as was stated earlier in this chapter, children themselves are causative agents. If they are allowed to develop of their own accord, they will produce a better society, with more freedom and more justice, with more democracy and resilience. The approach fits the agenda of present-day neoliberal policies: it transfers substantial duties from the state (as a duty-provider) to the individual citizens (as rights claimers) and expects the people themselves, including the children, through their own active claims to turn the potential rights into reality.

The ultimate question when dealing with poor children indeed is in what sense and to what extent the poor child in a poor family in a poor neighbourhood is an active change agent? In what sense should children participate, and in what sense should they fight for their rights? If we were to listen to those children, what message would they have for the adult? A close reading of the daily life of the children in poor communities across the developing world and of their vision for the future, as we will attempt in this book, may provide a useful input for the further discussion on involving children in development.

SUMMARY

In the wake of the CRC and its focus on child rights and child participation, agency of children in the development process has been highlighted by a number of scholars and by some of the more important child-centred development organisations, particularly by Save the Children. It has also been assumed that child is a culturally specific construction and that what children in developing countries are supposed to do shall not be imposed by Western-tainted norms of an ideal childhood. This approach which accentuates a different childhood for poor children in poor communities (in Third World countries), thereby expressing an anti-Western and an antiglobalisation stance, has a progressive ring to it. There are, however, many pitfalls associated with defending the idea of separate childhoods for different cultural hemispheres. Such an approach seeks out differences, and regards tradition as rather unchanging and homogeneous. It presumes that 'childhood' is a cultural construction, and empties it from the macroeconomic changes and long-haul historic processes. The so-called 'Western' ideas and ideals have penetrated daily life in the developing countries for ages and the official norm in those countries is akin to the universal childhood type as constructed in the CRC. Only detailed fieldwork, listening to the voice of the children, can establish whether indeed children in developing countries have different ideals, different norms, and different rights to claim. The voice of the children indeed will help us to unpack the concept of childhood and distinguish its universal commonalities and its local specificities.

Before one can comment on the impact of external changes on child agency, and the way in which children themselves have a proactive role to play, one needs to comprehend the ways in which the child socialises and at the same time actively contributes to the family and the social environment; and one has to determine how material poverty, mental deprivation, and disempowerment help to shape resilience and defiance, but also anger, distrust, and marginalisation. A problem with child rights in an abstract sense is that it tends to overlook the very serious constraints imposed by the asymmetric world order and the severe inequalities within countries. Children are social actors. Usually, they are less constrained by the contextual norms and expectations than adults, but, like adults, they live in an environment shaped by a defining social and economic structure. The location of the child's family within that structure, determines the parameters of childhood and the parameters of agency.

There is a need to explore this field and gain better insight into the potential of children under different circumstances. There is a need to know their priorities, their views of the future, their world view, their assessment of institutions and events. Understanding these aspects of the children is fundamental to child-centred projects. In the next pages of this book we intend to explore that vision and to understand how agency and structure interact.

2 Country Specific
Development Indicators, Child Conditions, and Research Areas

The following countries were selected for this study: Nicaragua, Bolivia, Burkina Faso, Tanzania, India, and Vietnam. There is a wide disparity in socioeconomic levels between these countries, which is made clear by table 2.1, in which a number of indices relating to the position of children in these countries are included. Burkina Faso is situated at one extreme of the scale (with high illiteracy, high child mortality, and high indices of child labour); Vietnam, despite a low GNP, is situated at the other extreme with a low fertility rate, a nearly perfect literacy rate, a reasonably low child labour rate, and a low infant mortality rate.

Absolute poverty is a condition characterised by the severe deprivation of basic human needs, including food, safe drinking water, sanitation facilities, health, shelter, education, and information. It is based not only on income but also on access to social services. The consequences are malnutrition, a high prevalence of diseases, high infant and child mortality, low life expectancy, low per capita income, poor quality housing, inadequate clothing, low technological utilisation, high unemployment, persistent environmental degradation, rural-urban migration, and poor communication. The effects of poverty on children are particularly intrusive in developing countries, since in quite a number of these countries, particularly in Africa and the Caribbean, children below the age of fifteen constitute 40% or more of the population.

In order to become a fully enfranchised citizen, with rights and obligations, a child must acquire knowledge and develop abilities and skills, particularly literacy and numeric skills. Tens of millions of children, despite a worldwide commitment to achieve universal primary education by 2015, still do not have access to education. Access to education is especially difficult for children living in rural areas and in urban slums, and for marginalised ethnic groups, for girls in particular. For those who do manage to enter the educational system, attendance becomes their new challenge; drop-out levels are unfortunately very high. In Burkina Faso, for example, only 36% of the children were enrolled in primary schools and only two-thirds of these children reached grade five. Net secondary enrolment was as low as 9% of all the children. Furthermore, the education received by many

Table 2.1 Child-Related Development Index (2003)

	Nicaragua	Bolivia	Burkina Faso	Tanzania	India	Vietnam
GNP (US $)	745	892	345	287	564	482
Parity GDP (US $)	3,262	2,589	1,174	621	2,670	2,490
HDI rank	112	113	175	164	127	108
Children (10–14) in Labour Force (%)	13	13	48	40	13	8
Fertility Rate 2000–2005	3.3	4.0	6.8	5.0	3.1	2.3
Male Adult (+ 15) Literacy	76.6	92.3	33.9	83.5	62.8	95.5
Female Adult (+ 15) Literacy	76.6	80.4	14.1	66.5	47.8	91.4
Infant Mortality Rate	30	53	107	104	63	19
Under 5 Mortality Rate	38	66	207	165	87	23
Male Life Expectancy	67.1	61.6	45.1	42.7	63.1	66.7
Female Life Expectancy	71.8	65.8	46.4	44.4	64.4	71.8
Population below 15 (%)	40.2	38.8	47.7	43.0	32.9	31.1
Population living with less than 2 $ per day	45.1	14.4	44.9	19.9	34.7	n.a.

Source: World Bank (World Development Report) and UNDP (Human Development Report)

children often does not give them even the most basic literacy skills. An unfriendly school system, which emphasises memorisation and mechanical learning, and which involves overcrowded classes without much teaching or infrastructural facilities, makes it next to impossible for boys and girls to achieve the very skills that they must acquire and develop to be full members of society.

Some countries have done better than others. Vietnam was the second country in the world to countersign the CRC, in February 1990, and of all the countries we studied, the children in Vietnam seem to have advanced most in terms of protection and care. Tanzania has unfortunately only been slipping backwards and Burkina Faso has maintained dramatically low levels.

2.1. VIETNAM

The Socialist Republic of Vietnam lies in the centre of Southeast Asia, with a 3,260 km long coastline, and shares borders with Laos, Cambodia, and China. Mountains cover three-fourths of its territory. It has a population of around eighty million. The population is unevenly distributed, with a high density in the Red River Delta, the Me Kong River Delta, and the eastern part of southern Vietnam. The country is inhabited by fifty-four ethnic groups, of which the Kinh (Vietnamese) are the majority, making up 86.8% of the total population. Ethnic minority groups live mainly in mountainous areas. Currently, one-third of the Vietnamese population is religious. Religions practiced in Vietnam are Buddhism, Christianity, Protestantism, Islam, and local religions. The natural population growth rate during the recent years has fallen rapidly from 2.3% in 1988 to 1.4% in 2000. The fertility rate, which in the mid-1970s was as high as 6.7, has come down to 2.3 births per woman. The sharp drop is a good indication of the success of the implementation of family planning programmes during the 1990s. The proportion of urban population has gradually increased from 20.1% of the total population in 1989 to 23.5% in 2000 (UNICEF Vietnam 2000; ICDS 1996).

Vietnam has had a long history of war and poverty, and the living standards remain low. Nevertheless, since the introduction of *doi moi* (the socialist market economy) in 1986, the country made significant progress, although this has unfortunately also resulted in accentuating the unequal development between city and countryside, between mountainous regions and plain areas, and it has led to considerable income differentials. Under *doi moi*, the share of industry in the GDP increased from 22% in 1980 to 35% at the end of the century, and the share of agriculture correspondingly decreased from 41% to around 24%. At the end of 2000, the GDP was more than double the level achieved in 1990. The extent of poverty has gradually declined. The food poverty rate, which was still 55% in 1990, was reduced to 20% in 1993 and 10% in recent years. The data on aggregate incomes, however, also indicate that the disparities between the urban and rural population have grown. There are also significant regional disparities. The Northern Highlands and the North Central coast regions are by far the poorest. These two regions, which are inhabited by 29% of the population, account for 40% of all the poor in Vietnam (UNICEF Vietnam 2000, 19). Ominous developments have also taken place, as the World Bank Report (quoted in UNICEF Vietnam 2000, 17–18) suggested:

> These findings suggest that doi moi has benefited the rich more than the poor and urban more than rural populations. . . . Social sector

reforms have removed traditional safety nets and instituted user fees for education, health care, child care and other basic services. These changes have undermined the ability of the poorest families to meet their children's basic needs, particularly in ethnic minority areas.

Child Conditions

In Vietnam, most communes and wards now have primary and basic secondary schools. Education used to be free, right up until grade twelve, but the social and economic reforms changed that, and now children must pay tuition fees and buy their own textbooks. Compulsory education for grades one through five was introduced in 1991. There was possibly no real need to make education compulsory at the time because most children (95% of both boys and girls) already attended school. Presently, the adult literacy rate is over 92%. Whereas the overall male–female literacy inequality in rural areas was 8.9%, it was only 1.6% in the age group 15–24, indicating that gender differences have largely abated as far as basic education is concerned. Of the ten-year-old children in the Red River Delta, 100% were attending school in the mid-1990s; in the Northern Uplands, it was only 91%, and in the Central Highlands it was even as low as 81% (Le Thi Quy 2003; Chinh 2000).

Since 1986, the health sector has improved considerably, along with the general growth of the economy. The state expenditure on health care in 2000 was 4.2 times more than in 1991. Efforts have been made to diversify the various types of health services: regional policlinics and a network of local health centres with important roles for preventive medicine and primary health care. Vietnam now has a better health infrastructure and better health indicators than most other countries in the region (see table

Table 2.2 Vietnam: Regional Comparison of Health Indicators

	Doctors (per 100,000)	Life Expectancy at Birth		Infant mortality rate		Fertility rate	
	2003	1970–1975	2003	1970–1975	2003	1970–1975	2003
Vietnam	54	50.3	69.0	112	19	6.7	2.3
Laos	61	40.4	54.3	145	82	6.2	4.8
Indonesia	16	49.2	66.6	104	31	5.2	2.4
Philippines	115	58.1	69.8	60	27	6.0	3.2
Thailand	30	59.5	69.1	74	24	5.0	1.9

Source: UNDP, Human Development Report 2004.

2.2). Infant mortality rate has fallen consistently from 46% in the period 1984–1989 to 19% in 2003. Similarly, the under-five mortality rate was 69%; it came down to 22% in 2003.

Research Areas

All three regions chosen for the study in Vietnam are located in the northern part of the country: Hanoi, Ha Nam, and Thai Nguyen (see Le Thi Quy 2003). These provinces represent three different types of regions in Vietnam: Phuc Xa precinct in Ba Dinh district (Hanoi) is an urban area, La Son commune in Binh Luc district (Ha Nam province) is found in the rural lowlands, and the Quang Son commune in Dong Hy district (Thai Nguyen province) lies in the midland mountainous area.

Hanoi, the capital city of Vietnam, has a population of four million people (2002), and is divided into several districts; Ba Dinh is one of the seven inner-city districts. It incorporates many historical venues such as the Ho Chi Minh Mausoleum, the National Assembly Building, and the Presidency Palace, but it has many poor wards as well. Phuc Xa, one such ward, is situated close to the Red River dyke (one of two greatest rivers in Vietnam). It has a population of approximately sixteen thousand people, of which 22% are children. A large number of immigrants live in this district. Manual labourers with a low income make up three-fourths of the population; their incomes fluctuate between 10,000 to 25,000 dong per day (15,000 dong = 1 US dollar). It has approximately one hundred drug addicts.

Ha Nam is one of the poorest provinces in the Red River Delta. Income is basically generated from agricultural activities. However, infertile soil, flooded rice fields, and year-round inundation are disadvantageous for cultivation. In Binh Luc, a district in the southeast of Ha Nam province, the average income per capita is 124,000 dong per month. Small-scale industries have been developing slowly, but many families have members who migrate to the cities in search of work during the agriculturally lean months of the year. In recent years, the poverty-alleviation programme in La Son has obtained good results; the share of families living in poverty has decreased to 7% of the population.

Quang Son, a midland and mountainous commune, has three main economic resources: the rice paddies, the tea plantations, and forestry. Tea planting has resulted in an increase in the general income and is now considered the main resource of the commune. This village has fifteen hamlets with around five hundred families of nine ethnic groups, mainly Kinh, Nung, and Hmong. The proportion of poverty-stricken people in 1998 was 26%. In 2001, this had dropped to 12%. All hamlets, except for one, have electricity, and 50% of the families have a TV. Health conditions have improved remarkably, thanks to the medical station which has two doctors and two nurses, and four sickrooms with eight sick beds.

2.2. INDIA

India has had a chequered economic policy since gaining independence from colonial rule in 1947. For a long time, it implemented an economic policy in which the state was supposed to steer the economy, to protect the indigenous market, and to benefit and subsidise the poor. In the 1970s this policy was known as the Garibi Hatao (remove poverty) policy of Indira Gandhi. In the 1980s and especially in the 1990s, the government took the road of liberalisation and integration in the world economy. Import tariffs were lowered, the regulation of foreign direct investment in many sectors was liberalised, and important state-owned industries were privatised. Since then, the economy has shown higher rates of growth but the growth was mainly on account of the service sector and of luxury goods and to some extent also in specific export-oriented sectors of the economy (such as the software industry around Bangalore).

The liberalisation generally did not generate much additional employment in the organised sector of the economy. Many of the protective social measures that hitherto had somewhat shielded the poor were scrapped, and poverty again started to increase in the midst of burgeoning consumerism among the elite. Whereas wealth has visibly grown in some of the cities like New Delhi, Mumbai, Hyderabad, and Bangalore, millions of people in many of the rural areas have not benefited from the economic reforms. About one quarter of the total population (250 to 300 million) is now estimated to be living below the official poverty line. The quality of life in the countryside has made only slight progress, at best. The lopsided development led to a further polarisation, with many regions being left behind, and it eventually brought about a wave of political discontent. After a couple of years of radical liberalisation during the government period of the right-wing Hindu party BJP, the Congress party has now come back to power with the support of the leftist parties and with a modified policy.

The country has the largest child population (375 million) in the world. Although many welcome changes have been achieved (such as the lowering of the infant mortality rates, an increase in child survival, an increase in literacy rates, and a fall in school drop-out rates), the achievement of compulsory primary education still remains elusive. A large number of children have to work for the survival of the family. Depending on the definition used, estimates on the magnitude of child labour vary from approximately ten million (the official government statistics) to one hundred million in the view of many NGOs (Lieten 2001 and 2004). Nearly 90% of all working children are found in rural areas; they are mainly engaged in agriculture and related activities. According to government sources, there are about two million children employed in hazardous industries, occupations, and processes.

Child Conditions

The educational statistics are a grim reminder of the glaring gap and the striking regional, gender, and caste differences that still exist in the Indian education system. Around fifty million children of the two hundred fifty million children in the age group of six to fourteen are still out of school. The female and male literacy rates in 2001 were 46% and 71% respectively, which compared very well with respectively 22% and 50% in 1981. The infant mortality rate, which was 126 (per 1000) in 1970, had come down to 61 in 2003, with great variations, ranging from 15 in Kerala to 98 in Orissa and Madhya Pradesh, and from 44 among the richest quintile to 109 among the poorest quintile (Kundu 2006, 23 and 34; Govinda 2002).

The sex ratio among children, according to the 2001 population census, has further declined from 945 in 1991 to 927 in 2001 for the zero- to six-year-olds, a glaring reflection of gender bias before and immediately after the birth of the child. In some more developed states like Delhi, Gujarat, Haryana, and Punjab, it is lower than nine hundred. Even though the country has a large buffer stock of food grain and runs the world's largest nutrition and feeding programme, almost 63% (approximately seventy-five million) children below the age of five are undernourished.

The population growth in India is an enormous problem. Whereas India had around three hundred million people around the time of Independence in 1947, today it has close to 1.1 billion people. Around 32% of that population is younger than fifteen, which puts an incredible strain on the educational system. In some states, particularly in the rural areas, the percentages are even higher. It is not that family planning is not being implemented though. Fertility rates have come down from 5.4 in 1975 to 3.0 at the beginning of this century. The increasing life span is one explanation for the population growth. Whereas people in 1975 on an average had a life span of only fifty, today the life expectancy has gone up to sixty-four.

RESEARCH AREAS

For the purpose of this study eight areas were chosen in four different states: the Govindpuri and G. P. Block Pitumpura slums in Delhi, the Film Nagar slum in Hyderabad city and Nalgonda District (Andhra Pradesh), the villages of Kalwari and Salempur in Muzaffarpur district (Bihar), and in Rajasthan the villages of Patan and Kotri in Ajmer district (see Lieten et al. 2005).

The slum dwellers of Hyderabad city and Delhi chiefly include rural migrants living in small, makeshift arrangements (*kutcha* shelters) with poor basic civic amenities such as sanitation, clean water, and electricity. Children constitute about 42% of the total population in the Delhi sample. The school enrolment ratio is fairly high at 80%, and there is almost complete enrolment in the lower age groups. While 60 to 70% of the enrolled children attend government schools, others attend either formal private schools or nonformal education centres. Despite the high enrolment, there is still a large proportion of working children (11%) and nowhere children (5–10%), i.e., children who in the official statistics are not accounted as child labourers but who are not attending school.

The state of Andhra Pradesh, with around 15% of the country's child labour force, has the highest number of child labourers in the country. Nalgonda district has one of the largest concentrations of child labourers. In the city of Hyderabad, Film Nagar, a relatively new slum, has a wide range of both traditional and new informal sector activities.

In the state of Bihar two villages, Kalwari and Salempur in Muzaffarpur district, were selected for the study. Kalwari is the larger village, with 485 households, and is more diversified in terms of caste composition and occupational structure. Salempur is a relatively small village with 315 households. Bihar is one of the most undeveloped states of India. With approximately 90% of its population residing in rural areas, it is also the most rural state of India. More than three-fourths of the population is dependent on agriculture, with a majority working as casual labourers. The state is known for lingering on of semifeudalism in its agricultural sector and for the caste-based social discrimination. The state has a population growth rate of 2.5%, which is higher than the other major states in India. The literacy level is the lowest among the major states. In 2000, the proportion of children 'not attending' an educational institution was as high as 43%, compared to the national level of 20%. However, the proportion of child workers in the state remains comparatively low, which implies that the proportion of 'nowhere children' is one of the highest in India.

The survey was carried out in two villages in the semidesert Ajmer district of Rajasthan, namely Patan and Kotri. Patan is relatively prosperous due to its proximity to Kisangarh town and therefore has access to diverse sources of livelihood. Kotri is a remote village with poor communication and infrastructure, and has limited sources of livelihood. Rajasthan, the westernmost state of India, is the largest state in terms of area and eighth largest in terms of population size. Although the literacy rates increased significantly to 61% in 2001, it still ranks low compared to other states. Rajasthan is characterised by a diverse landscape, ranging from desert and the semiarid regions of Western Rajasthan to the greener belts east of the Aravallis and to the hilly tribal tracts in the Southeast. Agriculture and livestock are the principal sources of livelihood. Hardship caused by drought has increased in recent years, mainly due to the loss of common property resources (communal land, pasturelands, and grasslands) by deforestation and encroachment. In spite of the increased literacy rate, educational deprivation, especially of women, continues to be high in almost all districts of Rajasthan. In the sample villages, nearly two-fifth of the population was literate (54.4% of the males and 25.7% of the females respectively). The health indicators are also among the poorest in the country.

2.3. BURKINA FASO

Burkina Faso is one the poorest countries in the world. As in many other countries in sub-Sahara Africa, particularly the children are hit by poverty and its consequences, e.g., malnutrition, poor health care, and the lack of education facilities. It is a landlocked Sahel country that shares borders with six countries along the Niger River. Three ecological zones divide the country: the semiarid Sahel in the north where the herding of animals is the traditional means of livelihood, the savannah plateau in the middle, an overpopulated area where most residents are subsistence farmers, and the humid south which has forests and savannah and a relatively rich soil. There are more than sixty distinct ethnic groups, many of them with their own distinct language. Quite a number of villages are multilingual. The dominant ethnic group, the Mossi, are scattered around the country; the Peul and the Tuareg people live in the north; the Lobi and the Goumanche in the south; and the Bobo in the southeast.

The average population density is thirty-eight per square kilometre, but most of Burkina Faso's eleven million people are squeezed into the agricultural area of the central Mossi plateau. Here, densities exceed two hundred per square kilometre. Rainfall is erratic and heavily concentrated in the summer months of May to September. Long periods of drought, frequent bush fires, and the traditional slash and burn agriculture have intensified land degradation, leading to desertification, particularly in the north. Over 80% of the population lives in the rural villages, and agriculture and livestock account for 40% of the country's GDP and for 60% of exports. According to the national analysis of poverty, 45% of the population is below the poverty line (INSD 1999). If one takes two dollars a day as the poverty level, a whopping 81% plunges under the poverty line.

Child Conditions

In 2005, Burkina Faso ranked 175th among 177 countries listed in the UNDP human development index. The total fertility rate in 1970 was 7.8; in the beginning of this millennium it was still 6.7 births per woman. The infant mortality rate and the under-five mortality rate remained high (respectively 107 and 207 per thousand live births) and life expectancy at birth (forty-five for males and forty-seven for females) was one of the lowest in Africa. Yet, due to the high fertility rate, the country's population growth rate remains high. It increased from 2.6% a year in the 1970s to presently 2.9% a year, enough to double the population in twenty years time.

Table 2.3 Education Indicators in Burkina Faso

	1994			1998		
	Urban	*Rural*	*Total*	*Urban*	*Rural*	*Total*
Literacy rate	51.6	11.8	18.9	50.6	10.8	18.4
Men	61.7	18.8	27.1	59.9	15.6	24.8
Women	40.9	5.7	11.4	42.0	6.8	12.9
Gross enrolment-primary	74.2	28.4	35.2	102.3	30.8	40.9
Boys	79.0	34.3	40.5	105.8	37.1	46.7
Girls	69.4	21.8	29.3	98.7	23.9	34.7
Gross enrolment-secondary	36.7	4.9	11.2	48.8	4.5	13.0
Boys	44.8	6.6	13.7	56.4	5.8	15.4
Girls	28.8	3.1	8.5	41.2	3.1	10.2

Source: Poverty Analysis Report-INSD-EP II—1999.

Primary school enrolment in Burkina Faso officially rose from 30% to 41% between 1990 and 2000, but retention rates and the corresponding progress in literacy have remained limited. The female and male literacy rates in rural areas in 1998 were only 6.8% and 15.6% respectively; as seen in table 2.3, the male literacy rates actually may have decreased during the 1990s. The gross primary enrolment rates, which anyway are a statistical measure which most likely is quite distinct from the net enrolment figures and even more distinct from the actual attendance figures, are still hovering around one-third of the child population. More than one-third of all children suffer from malnutrition. The development of the health indicators over time is also particularly disturbing. Between 1993 and 2000 conditions do not seem to have improved and may even have deteriorated. The health services indeed are still inadequate. Whereas Vietnam and India had fifty-four and fifty-one doctors per hundred thousand people, Burkina Faso, like many of its neighbouring countries, had only three doctors for as many people.

Research Areas

In Burkina Faso, two severely poor villages (Dem and Batie) were studied (Omer 2002). Most of the inhabitants work as sharecroppers or as casual village labourers. In other cases they migrate seasonally in search of work. A high proportion of what the villagers consume they produce themselves, except for a few essentials.

Dem is a small village in the Kaya province of northern Burkina Faso. It has a population of thirteen hundred people, predominantly Mossi, in approximately one hundred households. Due to its proximity to the Sahara, agricultural land is very scarce; a small lake near the village is a limited but valuable source of irrigation. The major crops (millet and maize) hardly satisfy the local consumption of the villagers. The limited land resources have pushed the younger population of Dem out towards the Ivory Coast to secure a living. Most families, with a few exceptions, have the same size of land and grow the same crops. There is a primary school in Dem with 140 boys and 100 girls. There are no local medical facilities and people have to travel two hours to the nearest medical centre. The most acute health problem is malnutrition. Some families eat twice a day, but the majority have to make do with only one meal.

Batie, with a population of around eight thousand, lies in the far southern part of Burkina near the Ivory Coast and Ghana borders. Batie comprises many ethnic groups, such as the Jolah, Mossi, Peul, Lobi, and Goumanche. It is bigger than Dem, both in size and population. It enjoys better social services, education, health, and transport. Because of its significance as a commercial area, Batie has been upgraded as the capital of a new province.

2.4. TANZANIA

The United Republic of Tanzania was formed in 1964 by the union of Tanganyika and the state of Zanzibar. The population on the island Zanzibar and the coastal regions of the mainland is predominantly Muslim, but Christianity is more prominent inland. Christians make up 45% of the population; 35% of the population is Muslim and the remaining 20% is Hindu or holds indigenous beliefs.

Tanzania has experienced a process of profound socioeconomic changes since independence. To speed up the development process, a model of state socialism based on village communities, known as *ujaama*, was introduced under the leadership of Nyerere shortly after independence. In the 1970s, Tanzania became famous for its achievements in the social sector, particularly concerning health and education. But the economy then entered a state of crisis. Living conditions deteriorated, dependence on donor aid sharply increased, and under IMF prodding, neoliberal market policies were introduced by the late 1980s. In spite of the policy changes, structural transformation of the economy and society has yet to take place; in fact, conditions appear to have gone from bad to worse. The GNP per capita, which in the early 1970s was US$280, had come down to US$240 by the end of the century. The quality of the health and educational systems declined and facilities could not be maintained. Agriculture remains as important as in the early days of independence, accounting for half of the GDP and 75% of exports; but industry, which had initially increased from 11% of added value in 1960 to 16% in 1990, has again fallen to only 14%. The various indices demonstrate the stagnant nature if not regression of the economy. About 90% of the arable land is farmed by smallholders on plots of less than two hectares, and the crops produced (mainly maize), are primarily for home consumption. It is estimated that about 6.6 million Tanzanians face chronic food insecurity, with the elderly poor, women, and children being affected the worst. Various sources indicate high levels of poverty and starvation. According to the Household Budget Survey of 2000–2001, 36% of the Tanzanian population fell below the basic poverty line and 19% below the food poverty line, compared to 39% and 22% in 1991–1992 (NBS 2001).

Poverty in Tanzania, together with the deterioration of the educational system and a worsening of the HIV/AIDS crisis, has also contributed to an increase in the number of child labourers. Because of the persistent poverty and the cutbacks in social services over the past decade, many parents have difficulties meeting the basic needs for their children, including food, school fees and materials. It is estimated that 3.4 million out of 12.1 million children in Tanzania under the age of eighteen, work on a regular basis and that one out of every three children in rural areas is economically active (IPEC 2002). Orphans are a newly emerging group of working children. It is estimated that at the end of 2001, close to a million children under the age of fifteen had lost their mother or father or both parents to AIDS. When the extended family system fails to accept orphans or fails to provide them with adequate care after the death of their parents, orphaned children are forced to move onto the streets where they have to work in order to survive. This group is especially vulnerable for child prostitution, one of the worst forms of child labour (FEB 2001, 127).

Child Conditions

Tanzania is among the poorest countries in the world, ranking 140th on the Human Development Index 2002, with a GNP per capita of US$210 and half of the population living below the poverty line. In many respects conditions in Tanzania around the end of the century were worse than in 1980. Population growth may have declined from 3.3% to 2.9% in the wake of a drop in fertility rate (from 6.8 in 1975 to 5.1 in 2003), but also because of a drop in life expectancy. Life expectancy had previously risen between 1960 and the early 1980s (for women from forty-three years to fifty-four years), but it then started to drop again. By 1999, female life expectancy had fallen to forty-seven years.

In the 1970s, the Tanzanian government started a programme for universal primary education (UPE) and launched a nationwide campaign for the construction of new primary schools. Within ten years, school enrolment tripled and at the peak of the UPE drive Tanzania had achieved a gross enrolment rate of 98% for primary education and gender differences were almost negligible. Since then overall enrolment rates have dropped dramatically. Today in Tanzania, less than half of all children complete primary school and only 6% make it to secondary school. Out of every one hundred children of primary school age, only fifty-six enrol in school. Only 6% of all the boys and 5% of all the girls proceed to the secondary school (Kuleana 1999, 12). More than two million children of primary school age are out of school (UNICEF 2002, 1).

The general health status of the population of Tanzania is poor. At the beginning of the millennium, it had an infant mortality rate of 104 per 1000 live births, an under-five mortality rate of 165 per 1000, a maternal mortality rate of 1,500 per 100,000 births and a life expectancy of forty-six years (compared to fifty years in the 1970s). A high percentage of deaths in Tanzania are caused by four poverty-related groups of diseases: infectious and parasitic diseases, illnesses of the respiratory system, nutrition-related diseases, and diseases of the digestive system. Malaria, acute respiratory infections, and diarrhoea are major contributors to high morbidity and mortality figures. But it is malnutrition that causes the most serious health problems for children. Nearly one-third of the Tanzanian children are moderately to severely malnourished. The greatest single cause of illness and death in Tanzania, accounting for at least one-quarter of all child deaths, is malaria. Another very important illness affecting children and youths is HIV/AIDS; there are 1.5 million people living with HIV/AIDS in Tanzania, of which 170,000 are children under fifteen (UNAIDS 2002; UNICEF 2002).

Research Areas

Three locations were selected in Tanzania: Mwanza, Ifakara, and Dar es Salaam, both its urban area and its agrarian hinterland (Reeuwijk 2004).

Mwanza, the second largest city in Tanzania, lies on the southern shores of Lake Victoria in northwest Tanzania. Two wards were selected from this city: the urban ward of Igogo in the city centre, and the rural ward of Mkolani, approximately thirty-five kilometres outside the city. The majority of the people in Igogo are self-employed, mostly in the service sector. Three-quarters of the population lives in unplanned settlements, usually in houses of poor quality on steep slopes and rocky hills. In these settlements there are little or no amenities such as electricity, water, roads, telephones, and so forth. The increase in population and economic activity has led to an increased demand for firewood, charcoal, and building poles, resulting in massive deforestation. In Mkolani most of the families own their own land, on average close to three acres. Most of the people have subsidiary jobs (95% of the men and 85% of the women), in addition to their primary job (which is mostly farming). The difference in income between Igogo and Mkolani is reflected in the consumer durables owned by the people. In urban Mwanza, most people have a watch or radio, with some having a television or even a refrigerator (15%). In Mkolani, on the other hand, quite a sizeable proportion of the inhabitants does not own any consumer durables (33%).

The Ifakara division lies in the Kilombero district of the Morogoro region, in southeast Tanzania. This is one of the country's most important agricultural areas. Roughly 80% of the district's population is engaged in agricultural activities. The major cash crop is rice and to a lesser extent sugar cane, cotton, cassava, cocoa, and fruits. On average, a family in Ifakara owns about 3.2 acres of land. We selected Lipangalala, Lumemo, and Kibaoni wards for research. The majority of the people in the first two wards are classified as very poor or poor. In Kibaoni more people are officially employed, mostly in small businesses. Selling beer is a popular subsidiary job in all areas. Health facilities are old and derelict. There is one doctor per thirty thousand inhabitants.

In urban Dar es Salaam, which has a population of over three million people, research was conducted in Buguruni and Vingunguti, not far from the international airport and near the city's largest dump. The incidence of very poor people is considerably lower than in the other research areas. Quite a number of people in these areas own a television and/or refrigerator (18%), 13% have at least a bicycle, and 48% own a watch and/or radio; however, around 21% of the respondents did not have any consumer durables at all. In rural Dar es Salaam, research was done in the Kibaha and Kisarawe wards. Both are agricultural villages, spread out over a considerable area. Major deforestation has taken place as a result of the need for firewood and agricultural land. The main economic activity in rural Dar es Salaam is agriculture, employing about 85% of the economically active population. Crops include cassava, maize, rice, sorghum, sweet potatoes, and bananas; any surplus of these crops is sold for cash. In rural Dar es Salaam, the four most serious problems are the water supply, the inaccessibility, the distances to the health facilities, and the bad conditions of the schools.

2.5. BOLIVIA

Bolivia is surrounded by Peru and Chile to the west, Argentina and Paraguay in the south, and Brazil in the east and the north. The country, despite its massive size, has only around 8.5 million people. Most of the inhabitants are relatively young: 39% of the population is younger than fifteen years. In the last twenty years, Bolivia has turned into an urban country: of the total population, around two-thirds live in the city and one-third in the countryside. It is the only country in Latin America with a majority of indigenous people. Only a 15% minority of the Bolivians consider themselves as 'white' Castellanos; the other 85% are mixed or indigenous people: 25% Aymara, 30% Quechua, and 30% mixed white/indigenous (Oostra and Malaver 2003, 27).

The Bolivian economy is characterised by the structural importance of agriculture and the mining industry, a strong dependency on foreign capital, and an ongoing struggle for the control of the natural gas and oil resources. Although Bolivia has, since centuries, been dependent on the export of raw minerals and agricultural products; it has imported most of its industrial products and semimanufactured goods. Its trading structure makes it especially sensitive to fluctuations in the world market. The limited industry that does exist in Bolivia was built in the time that the Bolivian government protected its own production by raising high taxes on imports (under the import-substitution policy). Under the neoliberal policies, which followed in the mid-1980s, many Bolivian companies went bankrupt. In some sectors (such as textiles), one could even speak of deindustrialisation (Oostra and Malaver 2003, 43). The privatisation and liberalisation policies led to the dismantling of the state economy, which had been built over the previous thirty years. The large informal sector worked like a sponge, absorbing evermore workers with low productivity and low wages in contrast to the modern sector of the economy. Under the new regime of President Morales, coinciding with a leftward shift in many countries in Latin America, neoliberal policies have been abandoned and the regime has brought in new policies that are aimed at reducing the hold of foreign companies on the national resources.

Although GNP per capita has tended to rise in the 1990s (to around US$900 in 2003), the increase was hardly one percent per year. Moreover, it does not have much effect on the poverty line. According to the official statistics, 63% of the people in 2003 lived below the poverty line. Some of the poverty was eased by food aid and food imports, but this in its turn undermined the viability of small farmers. A majority of the Bolivian population does not earn enough to meet basic needs. This has led to a situation in Bolivia in which 'most of the people work to be poor' (Grossman 2000). Poverty in Bolivia has a distinct ethnic colour. Most of the indigenous people live in the countryside where poverty is at its worst. It is also in the countryside that child mortality is exceptionally high, that life expectancy is low, and that education and social services are the worst. Therefore, 'the small, mainly white minority has a comfortable and luxurious life, whereas the small middle-class and the majority of the indigenous people's daily life is a constant struggle' (Oostra and Malaver 2003, 26). Political defiance from the left for many years landed the country in turmoil until 2005, when Morales, of non-Castellan descent, came to power on a wave of popular unrest. The new government has opted for a policy of marshalling the resources for a direct intervention against poverty, especially benefiting the indigenous population.

Child Conditions

According to the Human Development Index of the UNDP, Bolivia finds itself in the group of countries with a 'Medium Human Development'

(113th rank among 177 countries). The relatively low position is mainly the result of the indicators that determine the quality of life for Bolivian children, such as a high child mortality and low school enrolment. With a HDI of 0.687 in 2003, Bolivia was well below the average of the Latin-American continent, ahead of only Honduras, Guatemala, and Haiti. In 2002, the female and male literacy rates were respectively 81% and 93%; around 16% of the 2.7 million children did not attend school. The official net primary enrolment rate was 95%, but the statistics also show that those children who do enter the school system have trouble remaining there: 10% of the children who registered in the year 2000 dropped out. A high percentage of the children who manage to stay in school have difficulties in performing well: in the city only 30% of the children complete secondary school; in the countryside this percentage is only a poor 9% (UNDP 2002)!

In comparison with other countries on the Latin-American continent, Bolivia has faired badly in the area of health care. Life expectancy only reaches an average of sixty-two (61.1 years for men and 64.3 for women), whereas the average for the whole Latin-American continent is 69.6 years. According to the National Institute of Statistics, 37% of the Bolivian population received inadequate health care in 2001. In the rural districts of La Paz, Oruro, and Potosí the percentages were as high as 65%, 59%, and 60% respectively (INE 2001). The infant mortality rate is one of the highest of the continent: 53% in 2003 in comparison with 27% on the continent as a whole. The under-five mortality rate remains high (67% in 2002) and 10% of the children under five are actually severely underweight.

Research Areas

Bolivia is made up of three areas that are environmentally, socially, economically, and culturally are different from each other: the Highlands (Altiplano, 20% of the total area), the Valleys (Valles, 15% of the total area), and the Tropics (tropical, 60% of the total area).
The Altiplano is situated in the south of Bolivia and is often called the 'Roof of the Andes'. The Altiplano has the highest percentage of poor (67.6%), particularly in the western areas. Most inhabitants are from Aymara and Quechua descent. The main economic activities on the Altiplano are cattle breeding, mining, and agriculture, although the highlands are not really suited for agriculture; the climate is dry, the soil is not very fertile, the growth season is very short, and frost is a risk all year around. The city of El Alto and the rural village Chirapaca were selected for this study (Llamos 2001; Moreno 2001; Llamos and Moreno 2003).

Between the highlands and the tropical lowlands (1,000–3,000 metres) one finds the fertile grounds of the Valleys. Cochabamba was the urban selection for the study. Cochabamba has been a rich agricultural area ever since Inca times. The city itself is a dynamic trade centre with roads that connect the city to all corners of the country. Living conditions in the valleys differ greatly, from poor rural slums to wealthy agricultural areas where income is generated by cultivating rice, citrus, coffee, and coca. The village of Tarata was chosen to represent the rural areas of the Valleys (Llamos 2002).

The lowlands include the Bolivian Amazon and the dry Chaco area. The northern section of the Bolivian Amazon is witness to the cultivation of paranuts, the extraction of tropical wood, and extensive cattle breeding. In the *trópico séco*, the savannah of the Chaco, oil and gas are the main industries. Santa Cruz de La Sierra is the biggest city in the lowlands. It is Bolivia's primary city in terms of population and economic importance. Besides the booming agriculture and cattle breeding business, it is said that Santa Cruz is also favoured by the coca bonanza. The village El Torno was selected to represent the rural areas of the lowlands (Moreno 2002).

2.6. NICARAGUA

Nicaragua, hemmed in between Costa Rica, El Salvador, and Honduras, is considered to be the poorest country in Central America as well as the most indebted on the American continent. Throughout the twentieth century, armed conflict has played a significant role in the country's history. This has included twenty-three years of occupation by US military forces that supported the military dictatorship of the Somoza dynasty, which was in power from 1936 to 1979; eighteen years of armed civil unrest to overthrow that dictatorship; and eleven years of civil war after the Sandinista government came to power in 1979. In 1979 *Frente Sandinista de Liberación Nacional* set goals for the short-term solution of some social problems, including illiteracy and the lack of health services. But political polarisation and the counterinsurgency pushed the country to the brink of ruin again. The process of reconciliation after 1990 may have brought peace to the country, but it did not bring about improved living standards for the majority of the population, as rampant unemployment, illiteracy, violence, low health indicators, limited access to social services, and other difficulties continued to plague the country.

Years of structural crisis, war, hyperinflation, structural adjustment measures, and natural disasters have continued to exacerbate the conditions within the country. When structural adjustment policies were implemented at the beginning of the 1990s as a way to improve macroeconomic indicators, social programmes were reduced, contributing to the deterioration in the coverage and quality of health, education, and other public services. Almost half of the Nicaraguan population lives in poverty, a number of them even below the extreme poverty line. In the survey year, poverty among the rural population was as high as 76%. According to the international poverty line statistics, 45% lived on less than US$1 a day and 80% on less than US$2 a day, which left the majority of the population with one or more of their basic needs unsatisfied. Using other methodologies, the indicator of poverty is even higher.

Child Conditions

The Nicaraguan population increased at an annual rate of 2.7% in the 1990s, and reached approximately 5.5 million in 2002. The fertility rate has come down from 6.8 in 1970 to 3.3 in 2003, but this decline was not sufficient to halt the population increase or to redress the imbalance in the demographic structure. The demographic structure of Nicaragua represents a pyramid with a wide base: 38% of the population in 2005 was fifteen years or under, and the average age was seventeen (UNDP 2007).

Nicaragua is one of the countries in Central America with a sharp internal economic polarisation. Children, especially those under five years of age, are seriously affected by poverty: six of every ten children live in poverty and two of them live below the extreme poverty line. The demographic survey DHS (ENDESA 2001) shows that on an average 15.2% of children and adolescents between six and seventeen years of age were working: 3.4% in the age group six to nine, 12.8% in the ten to thirteen age group and 31.5% in the fourteen to seventeen age group. More than half of these children and adolescents were working at least thirty hours per week. In the UNDP index of Human Development it ranks 118th, just behind Bolivia and Honduras and just ahead of Guatemala. In the region, only Haiti is faring worse.

The adult illiteracy rate in 2000 was still as high as 33.5%. In 2001, 23% of children between seven and twelve years did not attend Primary School, and of the 77% attending school, only six out of ten completed the primary school. Drop out and repetition are the most common problems found in the primary school system. A total of 63% abandoned school during one of the six grades. Only 12% of Nicaraguan young men and women have access to further studies, currently offered by more than thirty universities, but seriously lacking financial resources, materials, and qualified academic staff. The children from poor families have to attend public schools, which lack just about all requirements or they fall outside the educational system because their families are unable to pay for their studies (school, clothing and shoes, books, utensils, monthly 'voluntary' quota, payment for tests, grade report and grade certificate, cost of transport and snacks, etc.). Instead, these children are frequently sent to work by their parents, in order to generate additional incomes.

Free access to health care is in the constitution, and Nicaragua is one of the big spenders in terms of health care (4.4% of GNP in 2000). Generally, access to health services is guaranteed, but 20% of the population, particularly in the Atlantic coastal and the central regions, is still not covered properly. Infant mortality and child mortality have decreased from respectively 113% and 165% in 1970 to respectively 30% and 38% in 2000. Yet, many of the children continue to suffer from chronic diseases and malnutrition. The official survey *Demografia y Salud en Nicaragua* calculated that 20% of the children below the age of five suffer from chronic malnutrition (Serra and Castillo 2003, 38).

Research Areas

In Nicaragua two urban and two rural areas were selected for the study. The urban areas included the Barrio Grenada in Managua, and the Barrio Jose Benito Escobar in Masatepe (Serra and Castillo 2003).

Masatepe, in the Carazo district, is a commercial hub in the midst of an agricultural area of coffee plantations, fruits orchards, cattle ranches, and corn and bean fields. The barrio has approximately 2500 families living in 350 overcrowded houses. It has a health centre and a kindergarten, thanks to foreign aid projects, but lacks a primary school.

Barrio Grenada, in Managua, is a local commercial centre which has attracted many rural immigrants, and now has approximately ten thousand inhabitants; most of them are living below the poverty line. In the late 1990s, the local health centre was dismantled and health conditions, which were already bad, deteriorated severely. Drug addiction, violence and gangs (*pandillas*) have led to a further deterioration of the quality of life. There are three small kindergartens, serving about one hundred infants, and only one primary school, which was initiated by an NGO (Plan International).

The rural municipality of Santa Rita lies at about 30 km from Masachapa. Almost half of its 750 inhabitants are younger than fifteen years. The soil is very fertile and many commercial products are cultivated, particularly sugar cane, vegetables, and fruits. The other selected village, Fatima, lies at about 2 km from Masatepe. Land reforms in the 1980s provided most of the families with small plots of land. Most of the 250 families cultivate coffee, fruits, beans, and corn.

CONCLUSION

The brief survey of the economic conditions and of the educational and health provisions in the six countries provides the background to our study. None of the countries, with the exception of Vietnam, have shown sustained improvements in the economic conditions which went to substantially reduce poverty levels. In fact the survey leads us to conclude that, particularly in the rural areas, a majority of the poorer families has found it increasingly difficult to survive. In general terms, GNP may have increased (although not in all countries), but the benefits have tended to be limited to the better-off sections of the society. The continuing use of children as an additional labour force, either to earn cash or to supplement household labour, appears to be one of the consequences.

In terms of health conditions, which have a direct effect on children, a fair degree of progress appears to have been achieved: infant and child mortality rates have indeed declined. The exceptions are Burkina Faso and Tanzania. In the latter country health conditions, represented by longevity, may have in fact degenerated. In all countries, despite a decrease in fertility levels, children account for a sizeable portion of the population, varying from 32% in Vietnam and India to 45% in Tanzania and even close to 50% in Burkina Faso.

In terms of literacy progress has been reasonable, particularly in Vietnam where universal enrolment at the primary level has been achieved. Primary education has made a fairly steady progress in Bolivia and Nicaragua as well. In India also, development has been significant, especially in view of the low enrolment rates of girls in rural areas even twenty years ago. Enrolment in rural areas of Burkina Faso, however, remains at very low levels; and in Tanzania, enrolment continues to decline.

The education system in all the countries copes with a number of problems, such as poor infrastructure. Due to the lack of funding, many schools are faced with such problems as overcrowding, inadequate sanitation and water, lack of staff houses, desks, tables, chairs, blackboards and other teaching materials. In addition the teaching is of poor quality. Many teachers in India, Tanzania, and Burkina Faso are poorly motivated to teach and consequently attend irregularly. Gender disparities are not particularly pronounced at the primary stage, but tend to increase during the higher stages of education.

A major problem, which should be addressed urgently, is the high dropout rate. It could be safely argued that most children enter the school system but that too many, for various reasons, do not continue and drop out either in the elementary stage or at the transition to secondary education. It is at that stage that, being inactive, they are at the risk of entering the labour market and becoming child labourers.

The choice of different research areas allows us to draw attention to the differences as well as the similarities of children living in urban areas, in well-connected rural areas and in remote areas; this will lend a wider significance to our conclusions.

3 Methodology

The assumptions that underlie our understanding of children in a specific area may not be correct for other regions of the world; in fact, they may not even be true for other areas on the same continent, or within the same country. Local cultures may show great variations and this may have a differential impact on the life of the children. Locations with different characteristics were therefore selected, so as to capture some of the variations that exist. In a country with a higher degree of urbanisation, such as Bolivia, more urban areas were selected. In a country with less urbanisation, such as India or Burkina Faso, more rural areas were included. Selections were made on the basis of differing socioeconomic characteristics. In each area, 150-odd households were supposed to be included in a socioeconomic survey. In the end, the sample was executed differently in different areas, and the number of families included in the study varied from 154 in Vietnam to 1224 families in India. In the selection of the families, the focus was on the poor households.

In each country, the procedure was similar: a background study, a survey study, and a qualitative study in the local context. The three levels allowed us to gain knowledge of the macroconditions, of family structures and conditions, and of the specific worlds of the children. The combination of survey work and microlevel anthropological research will help to assign some general validity to the detailed observations.

The sociological survey included data on child labour, education and welfare, and socio-economic and gender specific information about the material conditions in which children have to live. It also provided information on which the selection of families for the second and more intensive study of a limited number of poor children in each locality would be based. The data was generated from primary surveys of a sample of households. In India, for example, before conducting the survey, a complete listing of all households in the village was done in order to stratify the households on the basis of social variables. Then a random sample of households from each stratum was made to form the final sample of approximately 150 households in each locality. The survey was conducted on the basis of a structured questionnaire after it had been pretested in a pilot survey.

The purpose of the detailed study was to explore the microsetting of the household and understand the interactions between different household members. Particular issues concerning children were explored, e.g., their role in the family economy, their time allocation, their daily routine, their ranking of problems and their tasks, their likes and dislikes, their plans for the future, and their coping strategies. Children were also asked to reflect on their lives and their experiences.

Children between the ages of nine and fifteen were included in the study. The assumption was that beyond that age, children in many developing countries, particularly among the poorer sections, would have moved past adolescence and into adulthood. The justification of the lower age limit is that prior to the age of nine, the capacity of conceptualising and expressing ideas is less pronounced. The researchers were expected to stay in the neighbourhood of the children and to frequently meet with them so as to build up levels of trust. The children were to be studied for a total of three days. Revisiting the same children and keeping track of their various activities allowed the researcher to capture the various facets of daily life.

3.1. WITH CHILDREN

In theoretical debates on research methodology within social anthropology, it is generally agreed that it is difficult to represent the worldview of the Other, particularly when the Other is in a subordinate position. Poor rural or urban communities in Third World countries in general, and their women and children in particular, often have learned to live with asymmetric power relations, and in the confrontation with the outsider have taken refuge in the strategies of Silence and of Compliance. Being accepted as a trustworthy person, whom one can confide in, is therefore the first hurdle to be undertaken by the researcher, who also has to be aware of the perceptible and not so perceptible adjustment in behaviour and in the discourse of the respondents. Children learn how to handle the world of adults, and it should be assumed that they learn to handle the world of researchers as well. One could try to overcome this dilemma by frequently meeting with the child and doing so in an unassuming way.

The researcher, moreover, usually comes with an adult fieldwork style and with an overall ideological background that is difficult to shed. Even with anthropological tools and the intent to become as close to the children as possible, a gap will most likely persist between the different worlds. The following example illustrates this problem. After two weeks of fieldwork in an evening school in the popular neighbourhood *El 16 de Julio* in El Alto, in La Paz, we walked home with Edgar, an eleven-year-old boy whom we had come to know quite well. During the walk he revealed that he had joined a gang that operated in the same neighbourhood we were living. We asked with disbelief how he could have done such a thing. He listened to our arguments and then said, 'You are white, an adult, and from another country, and you think you can judge me? You just do not understand the way things work around here.' The initial shock resulted from the harsh realisation of the unbridgeable gap between us and of things happening without us noticing it. But then came the feeling that Edgar was willing to explain his behaviour and reveal his thoughts and that, rather than judging him, one ought to listen to his explanations as to *why* he joined the gang. Eventually, we told him he made a good point and that we would be grateful if he next time also could inform the adult *gringo* about 'the way things work here'. Edgar reminded us that the information one gets is mostly filtered and perforated. Yet, one can still try to bridge the gap between the different cultures (adult–child; foreigner–indigenous, male–female, rich–poor, intellectual–worker) by simply listening to the informants and remembering not to be misguided by preconceived values and typologies.

It should always be understood that children are encountered in a milieu embedded with institutionalised power relations. The school and the family are such institutions, which on a daily basis streamline children into normative social behaviour. These institutions are authorities to which the children must submit themselves. They expect compliance rather than defiance. It would therefore be helpful to meet the children outside this context as well as within this context so that also the noncompliant behaviour, feelings, and opinions can be observed. Different environments can be expected to play different roles in the unfolding of the child. The children, however, should also be observed in their formal educational surroundings, in which they learn their everyday skills, abilities, wisdom, and values. Access to children invariably involves the consent of the adults, such as teachers and parents. Moreover, adults themselves are an important source of information. Parents as well as other adult members in the household and in the community therefore will complement the information to be held from the research on children directly. But the children were the focus and the field workers were sensitive to creating an environment in which they could talk. Other techniques (for example drawing and observation) are helpful aids, but a careful registration of their narratives should not be abandoned.

The preliminary survey, which was conducted in each country, was of an exploratory nature, primarily aimed at gathering information about the socioeconomic background in the context of participation, needs and rights, the socialisation process of children, etc. The anthropological investigation that followed was carried out to complement the sociological part with qualitative data. In the sociological investigation quantitative research methods were used: a study of the available statistics, questionnaires, and formal interviews. The anthropological part on the other hand, mainly consisted of qualitative research methods: participant observation and informal and semiformal interviews.

Anthropological research can also help to verify the information that one already has. The added value of the anthropological method of investigation was made clear on a number of occasions. For example, during many initial conversations, children stated that they didn't work. However, when visits were made to the families, it appeared that some of these children *did* work; they were often found to be working together with family members (such as working with their fathers as plasterers, working in the shops of family members, working in the kitchen, etc.), but sometimes they were even found to be working for wages. They said that since they were only 'helping' their families and did not feel strained by the workload, they hadn't considered what they did as work. Another example is that many children appeared not to be working in the jobs in which they said they were working, probably because they were ashamed of the work they were actually doing. In addition, during initial conversations with the children we got many 'socially acceptable' answers about the institutions of socialisation, such as the schools and churches ('I like it very much'), and about their parents ('very good relationship'). Anthropological fieldwork allows the researcher to get more familiar with the particular child and the resulting data are therefore often more reliable than when using other methods.

3.2. IN THE FIELD

The research process in the six countries did not always follow the same route. Time constraints and interfering local circumstances were two significant interfering factors. In Bolivia, for example, the anthropological part of the fieldwork was first seriously hampered by a general strike, which blocked travelling in and out of the capital for many weeks, then by severe floods, and finally by a premature start of school holidays because of the early onset of winter, which meant that it became impossible to study the children whilst in school. In El Alto and Cochabamba, with Marten van den Berge of IREWOC, we conducted in-depth studies of four and eight families respectively. In El Torno the study was limited to semi-informal interviews with thirty-three children, without participant observation. This information was in addition to the sociological surveys, which had included six hundred families and had been conducted by colleagues of *Instituto de Investigaciones Sociologicas* (IDIS) of the Universidad Major of La Paz. Professor Danilo Paz of the *Universidad Mayor de San Andrés* (UMSA) of La Paz, and director of the IDIS, selected Antonio Moreno and David Llanos to supervise four groups of MA students to carry out the surveys. Together, they provided six reports on the separate research areas. The main findings of these reports were included in a general report (Llamos and Moreno 2003). All children involved in the study attended school. IDIS focussed on the children following evening classes, IREWOC included those who attended morning and day schools. All schools were public; no children from private schools were involved.

The studies in Nicaragua and India also followed the planned methodology. In Nicaragua, 160 families in four communities were selected. In each area, forty families were selected with a bias for poor and extremely poor households. A survey questionnaire was filled in during an interview with the head of the household. In addition, approximately twenty-five teachers and community leaders were approached as key informants and twenty children were selected for an in-depth study (five boys and five girls from both the age groups nine to twelve and thirteen to sixteen). They were observed in their environment (in the community, in school, in the family) and were engaged in discussions on various topics.

In India the study was conducted in four states, namely Andhra Pradesh, Bihar, Delhi, and Rajasthan. A detailed socioeconomic survey in Phase 1 covered 1224 sample households (of which 775 were rural households) covering more than of 6600 individuals in both rural and urban areas. Two villages or slums were selected in each state on the basis of crude development indicators like the size of the village, the proximity to urban centres, the ethnic concentration, and the incidence of child labour. In each of the eight areas around 150 households were covered through a structured interview schedule with open-ended qualitative questions. In each locality, six to seven children with diverse socioeconomic backgrounds were observed for three consecutive days by way of participant investigation. The researchers stayed close to the children, and built a rapport with them so as to make the children feel free to express themselves. In all, forty children were observed both from urban and rural areas. Separate case studies were prepared for each of the participating children. Village/slum profiles of the sample areas were prepared in order to contextualise the findings and to develop a broad socioeconomic profile of the sample areas. Focus group discussions and group interviews with children and parents, as well as interviews with local schoolteachers and staff of various child-centred organisations, were carried out as well. The majority of the households (55.2%) were poor, and 1.3% was even destitute.

The Vietnamese case study enriched the overall research design because the outcome of the study revealed the importance of the conditions within the family and the community, especially in terms of education, health, and poverty. Therefore, as our Vietnamese colleagues reminded us succinctly, research on children is impossible if it is separated from research into the family, community, and, ultimately, the role of the state in providing and protecting. Poverty has a multidimensional effect on the lives of children. All the children we studied, our Vietnamese partners reminded us, are all children (*tre-em*) with different degrees of confidence and protection, with sorrow and with joy, but they all had one common denomination: 'poor children' (*tre-em ngheo*). The research of the real-life conditions was a tall order, as it attempted to take into consideration the differential abilities of the children to cope with their conditions. Diverse methodologies, mainly sociological and anthropological, were used by the dynamic research team of the Democratic Youth Research Institute. Under the directorship of Le Thi Quy, three teams worked in Hanoi, Thai Nguyen, and Ha Nam. The researchers identified 154 poor households with children below the age of sixteen. They sampled and made a quantitative survey of 318 children (159 girls and 156 boys, with three missing cases); 37.7% were between nine and twelve, and 63.3% were between thirteen and sixteen years old. The researchers also conducted in-depth qualitative personal interviews with parents and with municipal leaders, school teachers, health workers, and staff of the cultural or childcare department. Interviews were also conducted with three groups at each site (one group of boys, one group of girls, and one group of parents). In order to regularly and closely monitor children's activities at school, in the family and in the community, the researchers moved into the households and kept diaries.

In Burkina Faso, family members belonging to 250 households were interviewed. A detailed questionnaire was canvassed with the assistance of a local research assistant. Consequently, fifteen families were selected for case studies in the first village, Dem, and twelve families were selected in Batie. Practically all the families were poor, literacy was minimal, the family size was very large, and two-parented households were not the standard. A large family size is the norm in Burkina Faso, and in Dem and Batie the average family size was even higher than the national average (9 compared to 6.7). Another distinctive factor is the polygamous nature of the household, as one household can consist of up to five wives living in the same compound with special economic arrangements. In the twenty-seven families, which we studied more closely, we counted as many as 264 children in the joint family system. Children were followed all day to monitor their activities, interactions among themselves and with the adult members of their families. Parents were interviewed separately to explore their perceptions about some important issues concerning their children e.g., education, future plans, household duties and responsibilities, etc. The investigation was done with less rigour than required and the analysis suffered.

In Tanzania, like in Burkina, research was conducted by IREWOC researchers. In each research area, 100 to 150 families were included in the socioeconomic survey, totalling 485 families. Socioeconomic profiles of the sample areas were developed, and the major problems facing the children were identified. During the second phase, focus group discussions with children were carried out to crosscheck and substantiate various inferences of the household survey. The majority of the 485 respondents (64%) were female. Of all families, 73% consisted of two parents, 14% were headed by a single woman; 58% were Muslim (mainly in Dar) and 36% were Christian. Most of the households were poor: in rural Dar and rural Mwanza none of the interviewees owned any luxury goods and the majority of people did not have any consumer durables at all. The Tanzanian anthropological sample heavily drew on school-going children, unlike the sample in Bolivia for example, which focussed on working children.

The researchers depended on transport provided by an NGO to reach the villages, which meant that they had to return home at the end of the working day, i.e., soon after the children came home from school. During interviews in the presence of the family adults, the children were very shy and most responses to our questions were '*I don't know*'. In contrast to these interviews, the group interviews conducted at schools or in the streets were extremely fruitful. On an average these focus groups consisted of four children between eight and fifteen years old; but during the interviews children who were passing by often became curious, stopped, listened, and then started to contribute. The main advantage of this method was that children encouraged each other to voice their opinions. Altogether, twelve useful in-depth interviews were conducted in Mwanza; ten in Ifakara and twelve in Dar es Salaam. The quotes were difficult to attribute to one specific child with one specific background, age, gender, class, or religion. The statements and views are best considered as group expressions.

The research in all areas has focussed on the poorest communities. The conditions of the neighbourhoods leave much to be desired: crowded and isolated housing, poor hygiene, often aggravated by a lack of water and the omnipresent garbage dumps with their swarms of flies and insects, and so forth. The lack of appropriate public services, especially those related to health, education, play and sports, is remarkable. Problems such as delinquency, vagrancy, and drugs proliferate in some of these communities, especially in urban areas of Bolivia and Nicaragua. Consequently, children and adolescents, as well as their families, under normal circumstances can barely satisfy their basic needs.

All the regions and their inhabitants included in the study face serious economic difficulties. This was found to especially be the case in Burkina Faso, rural India, and Tanzania. For example, in urban Mwanza (Tanzania), 93% of the respondents felt that their economic conditions were deteriorating. In rural and urban Dar es Salaam, a majority of the interviewees (74% and 69% respectively) felt that their economic condition was worsening substantially. People attributed their deteriorating conditions

Table 3.1 Perception of Economic Conditions in Tanzania

	Worse	*Stable*	*Better*
Rural Dar	74%	13%	13%
Urban Dar	69%	16%	15%
Ifakara	66%	11%	23%
Urban Mwanza	93%	0%	7%
Rural Mwanza	86%	4%	10%
Average	74%	11%	15%

and declining entitlements to inflation, higher prices, and irregular sources of income. The levels of poverty also informed us about the effects of globalisation in the sense that in the field the obvious impression was that economic fortunes had not improved and that employment prospects in the formal sector, particularly in government service, had declined. The net effect of this on children was not only that they continued to live in poverty, but that in some areas like in Tanzania possibly in increasing poverty, and that prospects for the future were not really attractive.

After having provided an idea of the areas in which the field work has been conducted and of the methodology used for collecting the data, we now move to the more substantial chapters and shall look at three realms in which the children operate: leisure, work, and education.

4   Leisure and Daily Life

In this chapter we shall describe what children do during the day and how the socioeconomic conditions they live in affect their options and choices. Children by and large operate in four different spaces: *the home compound, the school compound, the school access route, and the roaming area*. The last in that list is somewhat limited for the children living in cities, as their habitat has mostly grown into urban jungle. Urban people witness the mushrooming of new hotels, roadside shops and houses, but unfortunately not the development of many schools or cultural and sport clubs for children. A potential fifth space to add to the list above, one which would be greatly beneficial to children, is regrettably unavailable to most: playgrounds or cultural and sport centres. Playgrounds for children in most areas are a luxury.

In this chapter, we shall look at the home compound, and somewhat also include the roaming area, i.e., the time and place for play and leisure.

4.1. PLAY AND LEISURE

Children make different choices about what to do during their free time. The leisure activities of the children in the Vietnam study were carefully registered and the results are summarised in table 4.1.

The table shows the children spend most of their free time playing with friends. Watching TV is the second activity that children most like to do, both in urban and rural Vietnam. Children watch TV at home or go to their neighbours if their families cannot afford a TV set. TV programmes have improved and have diversified with education in mind. Besides programmes for children including films and circus shows, there are plenty of educational programmes, such as those that teach foreign languages. The content of the programmes is in sharp contrast with what is offered in for example India and Nicaragua.

Television and Internet have a great educational potential and can offer access to new cultures and new opportunities, but unfortunately shallow entertainment dominates, which is particularly regrettable from

Table 4.1 Children's Activities During Free Time in Vietnam (%)

	Daily	Sometimes	Don't do	No answer
Watch TV, video	48.7	44.7	4.7	0.0
Listening to radio	13.2	33.6	34.9	18.2
Reading a book or newspaper	31.8	42.5	13.2	12.6
Playing sports	20.8	40.3	23.9	15.1
Playing computer games	3.8	11.3	62.9	22.0
Playing with friends	52.2	40.6	1.3	6.0
Sleeping	9.4	48.1	26.4	16.0

a pedagogical point of view. The media with so much potential fails as a healthy pastime that can help develop children's mental and physical power; in fact, children are more likely to be negatively influenced by the overload of Western-inspired pop music, violence, and erotic images. In Nicaragua, 75% of the children are regular television watchers, and 45% listen to the radio. Only 10% read newspapers, and even then mainly the sports and humour sections. Favourites on television include cartoons and *telenovelas*, the soap programmes. The reasons the children give for their preferences are varied: 'suited to my age', 'it entertains', 'it keeps us off the streets', 'learning important things'. The children think that programmes should entertain and inform, although many enjoy the cartoon *Pokemon* because of its violence. Most of the programmes shown on the various channels, with few exceptions, either douse the viewers with the banalities of an illusory world, or are riddled with violence and eroticism. The exposure to television is usually not curtailed by parents. Children remarked frequently that it would be good if television could expand on the themes that come up during school hours, such as the drugs problem, and protection against other social problems and dangers. Miguel Ángel Flores (fifteen years old) gave the following example: 'The programme *Sixth Sense* on Channel 2 was such a good programme; it helped to inform and to present problems for all youngsters to enjoy, too bad it is gone'.

TV in Indian cities within a short period appears to have developed into a new addiction, especially for dropouts from school. Jyothi (twelve) in Hyderabad stopped going to school because her parents claimed that they could not pay the school fees. She would have loved to continue school because there she was learning how to read and write, and hoped to later become a doctor and treat ailments such as asthma, from which she herself suffers. She is a typical 'nowhere child': she is neither in school nor in the workplace. Her entire day consists of playing, watching TV, and doing small errands. She usually wakes at 7:00 a.m.; after washing and breakfast she plays with her sisters and cousin. They play in the sand, making sand cakes, and run around until 1:30 p.m., which is when the mother and grand-mother come back. They then all have a lunch consisting of rice and lentils, identical to their breakfast. Jyothi then sleeps for one hour and then sits in front of the TV and watches soaps until about 5:00 p.m., which is when her mother asks her to go and have a bath. After getting dressed she starts playing outside the house in the mud with her sister until 6:30 p.m.; she then comes inside to watch TV again, and goes to sleep at 8:30 p.m. after eating her dinner.

The next day is not much different; the only change is that she visits her neighbour who has cable television, and they watch a movie on the com-mercial channel. At 2:00 p.m., she comes back to her house and has lunch, which again consists of rice and lentils. At 2:30 p.m. her mother switches on the TV and Jyothi sits on the bed and watches Telugu shows again. At 4:00 p.m. her mother tells her to go and get some shampoo from the shop so that she can wash her hair. After eating some more lunch with her mother, this time including a leafy vegetable, she again goes outside the house and starts playing with her friends until 7:00 p.m. She then comes home for dinner, watches television, and falls asleep at 9:00 p.m.

In Vietnam, where school attendance is extremely high, the rate of children participating in daily sports activities is low, only around 20%. This is not because they don't like sports but because they don't have the equipment. Whereas urban children lack playgrounds and space, rural chil-dren lack equipment and facilities. Children in rural areas often resort to makeshift solutions, such as making a football from wrapped-up cloth. When cultural and sport activities, like bike racing, Ping-Pong, football, and badminton, are organised for children during festivals or holidays, the children respond enthusiastically. They agree that such activities should be held more often; the secretary of Youth Union in Phuc Xa district stated: 'What we have been able to organise does not meet the demand because those kinds of games are not held frequently enough. We are lacking of money and people to do this'.

Such apologies were common. The study found that the adults in the communities throughout the countries do not stimulate conditions for chil-dren and adolescents to practice sports and enjoy healthy leisure. Parks and squares in rural communities are lacking and those in urban neighbour-hoods are badly maintained. According to the children in Nicaragua and Bolivia, one of the things they dislike most in their neighbourhood is the lack of entertainment and the absence of sport facilities. In other areas, the idea of sport facilities had not even entered the imagination. Most of the children's play is done close to home, but parents don't always facili-tate this. They often find the children and their playing bothersome, and instead of offering creative guidance they scold and punish the children. In Quang Son, some parents were clearly not pleased with boys playing at midday, since for adults it is the time to rest. The children's play is noisy, resulting in irritated parents and the children ended up playing out in the rice fields or forests:

> We only play games while tending buffaloes in the fields away from home. It is because if we had quarrels or were too noisy, parents would scold us and sometimes beat us. (Interview with a group of boys in Quang Son)

To illustrate the typical choices made by children during their free time, a case study has been set out below. The case shows the exact activities of an eleven-year-old schoolboy during one day. Trieu Van G., a seventh grader in Quang Son commune, almost every day tends the cows or does some cleaning work around the house for, on an average, less than two hours a day. His work is light and simple, suitable to his age. He also goes to school but still has a fair amount of spare time. He gets up at six, and half an hour later goes to school and comes back at twelve, when he has lunch and watches television at his uncle's house. Between 1:30 and 5:30 he takes the buffalo to different grazing sides and in between plays with his friend. The total working time tethering the buffalo is almost one hour. Work in this case was very much intertwined with playing. Trieu was responsible for the buffalo for the entire afternoon, and he took that task seriously, but in the meantime he very much enjoyed playing around with his friends. When he returns home, he helps in preparing dinner for half an hour and then watches television for twenty minutes before having a bath and washing his clothes. Afterwards he has his dinner and at 7:30 starts on his home work; at nine he goes to watch television at his uncle's house for one hour and then goes to bed. At the end of the day, Trieu can look back on a day in which he attended school (and finished his homework), did some playing with his friend at a safe distance from the adults, and took his responsibility in contributing to the household economy by looking after the buffalo and assisting in the kitchen.

4.2. WITHIN THE FAMILY

Adultism is the attitude towards children whereby they are considered as objects owned by parents or adult guardians; they are treated as if unable to think and to distinguish right from wrong and make decisions. Consequently, the children are kept in a subordinate position until they reach the legal age of adulthood. Spending time in the playground or other spaces beyond the sight and out of earshot of adults is therefore crucial to a sound childhood in which the child can develop its autonomy and its networks and in which it can allow the imagination and the practical understanding of the world to develop.

The family is the main organisational unit of the economic, social, and affective lives of people. It is the unit around which the life of the child revolves. The majority of the children were satisfied with the environment at home, but the study also observed (in Tanzania, Bolivia, and Nicaragua) that many families were affected by break-up processes, such as divorces, abandonment by one or both parents, poverty, unemployment, alcoholism, violence, and the crisis of moral values. Whether it was in defective families or in normally constituted families, at home, children are continuously faced by demands by adults. That is one of the reasons why children like to go to school or to go and play outside. There they can spend time with peers and friends. This is one of the great opportunities which the school offers to the young kids. Social contacts through school, especially outside the classroom, offer an escape from adultism, which is imposed on them whenever they are on adult territory (inside classroom, home, workplace, etc.).

One-fifth of the sample in Nicaragua expressed negative views of their families: they dislike the quarrels of the family members, they are not allowed to play, and they are verbally mistreated and beaten by family members. This suggests an extensive social problem of child abuse. The same children wished that their parents (or guardians) would have a more positive attitude, giving them confidence, advice and freedom, and that they were more loving, understanding, and accommodating. In quite a number of families children indeed appear to be the property of the parents. They are not regarded as people with their own rights but rather as a source of danger that constantly needs to be controlled and as an extra hand in the household. The children clearly become distressed when relations within the family are in discord. When conflicts do take place, the children often choose to respond with silence and avoidance. They know that if they get involved they are likely to be reprimanded or, even worse, physically punished.

Many adults believe that physical punishment is the appropriate method to correct children when they are disobedient, lazy, or argumentative. In addition to verbal mistreatment, the most traditional methods of punishment by adults involve the belt, the rope, the whip, and the stick. In our study in Nicaragua, half (52%) of the parents admitted to having used violent forms (shouting, beating) in order to discipline the children; other parents (11%) said they punish their children through restrictions (e.g., no TV, no playtime); and others (37%) claimed that they use dialogue and discussion. Our study in Vietnam indicated that many parents still think that it is necessary to apply physical punishments.

To find out more about the extent of violence used against children, we asked the children about beatings they had experienced. In Vietnam, as many as 82% of the children said they were scolded and beaten, of which 67% said the parents had done the beating. Others reported beatings by relatives and even by school teachers. One girl said, 'I fear my father the most. Each time he beats me I feel as if my skin is being peeled off. I am very much afraid of my elder brother because he often beats me and I feel a lot of pain.' Most of the parents acknowledged that beating was legitimate. A parent in La Son stated:

Yes, I do beat them when they are insolent and stubborn. Only when they are scolded and beaten, they will be frightened. When they are scolded and beaten they keep silent and work. If we don't scold them they will be lazy and do nothing. We should be more careful in educating daughters. We should scold and beat them to make them mature.

The ambivalence within the family is clear. To the children the family is a source of survival, protection, and reciprocal help, but it is also a place where power relations are exerted. The household is a group of people who produce and consume in common; they share their resources and allocate the work according to sex, seniority, and convenience. The adults in the family generally determine how children divide their time between school, work, and free time. The household may provide children with protection and support but many children indicated that punishment for misbehaving is always looming. Addou (eleven) from Dem (Burkina Faso) was referring to this hazard when he said: 'Many things I do not want to do but I just do them out of fear; my parents would give more tasks if I refuse to do something as required.'

Children in a way depend on parents to manage their time. They are told what to do, when to do it and how to do it. Their time at home is shaped by family routines and decided upon by the parents; children are rarely asked for their opinions on the matter. 'Not being given the opportunity to say what I think', was a frustration expressed by many of the children, of all ages. In the long run, if the child is not given enough room to manoeuvre and to act on its own, a mental frame of domination and submission will be reproduced. In this sense, the family space may also standardise adultism and gendered injustice, restricting the capacities of boys and girls within a traditional culture of expectations.

The family plays an irreplaceable role in socialisation, material survival, and the satisfaction of the emotional needs of children and adolescents. Despite grumblings about adultism, the children generally also expressed appreciation of the love and protection they receive, as well as the teachings of their parents, the support, the authority, and even the discipline. In the households, we found that the relationship between children and parents is generally loving, co-operative and respectful. The parents only wish the best for their children and therefore try to make them study and 'learn how to earn a livelihood'.

Children have a fair perception of reality. They are usually found to be sensitive to and understanding of difficulties resulting from the economic situation of the family. They contribute wherever they can by performing different household and agricultural tasks, or even going elsewhere to work. They are assisting and cooperating in tasks assigned by adults and that actually is what 'participation' is about.

School-going children in most countries do not have much free time, particularly during the school year. Most of their time is spent in school,

Table 4.2 Children's Play Time (%) in Vietnam

	During school year	During summer holidays
Less than one hour	17.9	6.3
1–2 hours	51.5	7.7
3–4 hours	25.7	33.7
Over 4 hours	4.9	52.3

on homework, or on household chores and related activities. In Vietnam we calculated that, during the school year, more than two-thirds of the children have less than two hours a day for playing, and only 5% play for more than four hours.

In most cases the majority of the girls conduct simple work such as housework, childcare, and some other odd jobs. This holds true for many provinces in Vietnam, especially in rural and mountainous areas. Let us look at a typical school day in January of fifteen-year-old Pham Huyen T., tenth grader, from Phuc Xa. T. has thirty minutes a day for a quick nap, and twenty-five minutes for playing. On a day off, she goes to her friends' houses or plays with her younger siblings for about an hour. Individual cases may show a different pattern.

Box 4.1 A Day in the Life of T.

0600	Gets up
0600	Washes face and has breakfast
0635	School
1230	Lunch
1300	A short nap
1330	Tutorial class
1615	Plays with younger sister and brother
1640	Helps father to prepare dinner. Her mother sells fruits and vegetables from 0500–2300
1705	Takes a meal to her mother
1730	Dinner
1800	Washes dishes and cleans the house
1830	Attends to her ninety-year-old grandmother
1920	Studies and teaches her younger siblings
2205	Goes to bed

As the children grow up, they are expected to take on more household responsibilities. Most children said that their free time is increasingly limited as they grow up. An appreciation of their families' situation, love, and a sense of solidarity, makes them feel more and more responsible to work in support of their families. Children have been taught, or have learned from the behaviour of others, that one ought to contribute in the household, in addition to working hard at school. Between school and home not much time remains for leisure activities. As Nguyen Thi L., a girl aged twelve, from Phuc Xa ward, complained: 'I wish that the workload in school be reduced so that we have a little more time to play. I am very tired, because after school I have to take extra classes.'

Most of the interviewed children and adolescents enjoy being able to help the family, to learn new things, and to sometimes earn extra money. This positive attitude is one of solidarity and responsibility, but such daily chores may negatively affect performances in school. To get an idea of what tasks children perform in the households and of the solidarity experienced by children in respect to household survival, let us look at an example from Tanzania.

A typical weekday for the children we interviewed in one of the rural areas of Tanzania begins at 6:00 a.m. with bathing, breakfast or a cup of tea, washing dishes and sometimes fetching water before school, which starts at 7 a.m. When school finishes at 2:30 p.m., children return home and do household jobs. Household jobs mostly comprise of fetching water and firewood, cleaning dishes, sweeping the house, washing clothes, taking care of siblings, cooking, etc. Helping parents or other family members with their jobs is regarded as a household chore because the children do not get paid for it. For children in urban areas, this mostly means that many help their parents with selling products and doing small business; for most children in rural areas this involves helping with farm work and/or fishing. On average they spend about three hours helping in the household. When those chores are done they play and/or do homework for another two hours, followed by dinner and bedtime at 9:00 p.m. During the weekend children normally help their families with the family business or farm on a full-time basis and some children also spend some time on paid jobs.

During one of the group interviews it was stated that '*the older you become, the more responsibilities you get in the household.*' This was stated as if it was a universal fact and the children indeed did not seem to have much trouble with the amount of energy and time they had to invest in fulfilling their responsibilities and household jobs. Only a few times, mainly in rural Mwanza, it was mentioned that they sometimes lack time and/or energy for doing homework or playing with other children, having just completed their school and household responsibilities. Work in the case of some of these children prevented them from living the normal life of a local child. Such claims on children usually occurred in broken families.

The story of Esther (fourteen years old, currently in standard seven, the eldest of three children with divorced parents) is typical:

> When I wake up in the morning at 6:00, I have to clean the house and its surroundings. At 6:30, if there is no water, I have to fetch water before going to school at 7:00 a.m. At 2:00 p.m. I come back home from school. After lunch, it depends. Sometimes I do some homework, and if my mother is not around I have to do all household jobs. Actually just now I am going to wash my clothes. If there is enough time left, I will do my homework. I also take care of my younger siblings. Then later in the evening at 6:00 p.m., I am going to the market to help my mother sell fish and tomatoes. I shall stay there until 9:30 p.m. I usually have my dinner at 10 o'clock and then I go to bed. I also may make some money, but not much, if I do some embroidery and then I sell these clothes. This is the only way to get money.

4.3. CHILDREN IN THE INDIAN COUNTRYSIDE

Below are two cases in which children's activities were observed during one day. The cases are of children in the Indian countryside and do illustrate how the life of the child is embedded in local institutions. The children go to school but since schools are of substandard quality, attending or not attending school on a daily basis is not perceived as necessary or useful. There are many more useful things to be done, like assisting in the household or looking after the cattle. Since such work very much combines with leisure time, it is difficult to classify these children as child labourers. They indeed are working many hours per day, but such work is of a light nature and is done intermitted with playing and enjoying, taking time off for all kind of interesting side activities. The discipline, which an efficiently run educational system should extract from the children is missing. Although many of these children may go to school, and moreover spend time on tuition and homework, the perception which they and their parents, possibly also the teachers, have is that school can be foregone on any day of the week when other obligations arise.

The first case is that of Ashok Ram, one of the boys whom we followed in a poor village in Bihar in the eastern part of the country. Ashok, eleven years old, is the youngest child in a family with many working siblings. The family is not too poor: it has 2.5 acres of land, two bulls, a buffalo, and income from agriculture and nonagricultural wage earning. Yet, mainly due to illnesses in the family, they have to struggle for food all year round. They live in the Chamar-toli, the residential area of the lowest caste families. Ashok is an interesting case to start with because his daily activities illustrate the difficulty of separating leisure, study, and work. On the first day of observation, the boy worked for around four to five hours, including

Box 4.2 A Day in the Life of Ashok

0530   Ashok has just woken up and is tying first the buffalo and then the bull near a tub outside his house. Then he goes to have his morning rituals in the field with a mug of water in his hand. He is wearing worn-out trousers and is barefoot.

0600   After going to the toilet, he provides fodder to the animals and cleans the outer part of the home. While the animals are eating, Ashok is cleaning the floor with cow dung. Then he brushes his teeth and cleans his mouth and hands.

0700   Completing the homework given in school, namely the additions and subtractions given by his teacher, and copying the sentence 'Ram is a good boy' in his notebook several times. He is then called from within the house. Leaving his books, he goes inside and comes back with his crying nephew in his lap. Around fifteen minutes later Ashok's tutor arrives. Ashok leaves his nephew inside and comes out for tuition for which four other students have also come.

0800   During tuition, the teacher corrects the mistakes of subtraction and explains them through examples. Ashok easily solves the sums but is facing problems with subtractions.

0900   After tuition Ashok takes the bucket, mug, and towel and goes to the hand pump to take a bath. He then goes inside his house and puts on his shirt and pants and then sits down to have his food. In a small steel plate he is served four *chappati*, vegetables, and salt. Ashok finishes his food and places the plate near the pump.

0945   Before going to school, Ashok is reminded by his mother to come back early from school since his elder brother has gone out and he has to work in the field.

1000   As soon as the bell rings, all the students stand in a queue with joined hands and start prayer. Finishing the prayer, students go to their classrooms and the teachers to the office. Ashok goes to the second form. He sits in the third row on the concrete floor. The roof and the blackboard of the classroom are in bad shape. There are about thirty to thirty-five girls and fifteen boys present in the classroom. At about 1045 the teacher comes in and children stand up as the teacher enters and sit down as soon as commanded by the teacher.

1045   After registering the attendance, the teacher starts explaining sums. She asks the students to do the sum of 15+12. When the bell rings, she gives new sums (23+14 and 34+22) for the next day, and leaves the class. The students start talking to each other. A new teacher arrives.

1115   The teacher writes five flower names on the board and asks the students to copy them and to write names of five cities. Ashok copies the names of five flowers but he cannot write the names of five cities. The teacher pays little attention to the pupils.

1200   This time kids are more excited as soon as the next teacher, Pushpa madam, enters the class. She explains about the Dussehra festival and enquires about the children's plan for this festival. Most of the students appear happy and are talking to the teacher openly. After the bell rings,

(continued)

Box 4.2 One Day in the Life of Ashok *(continued)*

the teacher wishes the children a happy Dussehra festival and tells them to refrain from naughty activities.

1245   While the boys and the girls in the class are talking about Durga Puja, the new teacher arrives and tells the students to write the numerals from one to hundred. As the bell rings for lunch, Ashok leaves for home.

1330   On the way home, he says that Pushpa madam is the only madam who teaches while Asha madam beats them; most children like Pushpa madam very much because she is so affectionate while teaching. Reaching home he changes into an old shirt (torn) and pants. He is given dry *chappati* and salt which he eats immediately.

1400   He is taking care of the young kids and playing with them, as asked by his mother. Simultaneously, Ashok is trying to do some other work e.g., cleaning the cow shelter but this is made difficult by the crying kids which he then hands over to his sister in-law inside the house. He then goes to his sister who is cutting grass nearby.

1500   He joins his sister in cutting the grass and soon fills up the basket and brings the cut grass home, where he thrashes it to remove the dust. He cuts the grass with his cutting machine and serves it to the animals. Then he cleans the cow shelter with a broom.

1600   Ashok patiently and slowly cleans the place. Then he gives fodder to the animals. His sister comes with her son asking him to take care of him. Keeping his nephew in his lap he fills the tubs several times with fodder and water. In the meantime, the kid has soiled himself and Ashok has to clean him.

1700   Ashok plays hide-and-seek with his friends near his home. In between he also looks after the animals. In this game one player has to put a blindfold over his eyes and he has to catch hold of another player and identify him. After playing and feeding the animals Ashok starts on his studies.

1830   Ashok goes to the outer part of home where male members generally live, with a lantern and a bag to study. His brother and father are talking about the family problems. None of the members of the family pays any attention to what he is studying. Ashok himself listens to the story of a court case which is to take place the next day.

1930   After he finishes, Ashok comes inside the home, washes his hands and mouth with a mug containing water, and eats the food served by his mother: rice, potato, and eggplant. The family members discuss the court case. The elder brother was married two to three years back but relations got strained and the in-laws filed a lawsuit against his brother under the Dowry Act and charged him with atrocities. Ashok goes to bed after finishing his food.

2045   Ashok is asleep.

the responsibility for the cattle, the support to his sister in cutting grass, and the baby-sitting, but this work apparently interfered neither with his studies (he was in school for four hours and spent two hours on housework) nor with his leisure time.

The next day Ashok's life is different. The early morning practice is similar though, including the session with the tutor. The tutor thinks greatly of Ashok and believes that he will do well in his studies. The rest of the family is generally uninterested in Ashok's schooling. After the tutor leaves, Ashok goes to the field and weeds and collects fodder for the animals. When asked why he isn't going to school Ashok replies 'there is work to be done: weeding, collecting grass, and preparing the field for maize seeding.' His father asked him to not go to school; Ashok understands the feelings of his family. He does the work that is assigned to him, responsibly and willingly. During his time for rest (1200–1400), he explains that due to poverty he cannot go to school regularly. When members of his family go to the field, he has to take care of the children at home. He has a desire to study but due to his family responsibilities he cannot fully concentrate. Ashok wants to be a policeman after his studies. Ashok loves watching TV at some distant neighbour's house; apart from religious serials, he also likes *Hello Inspector*, and he has seen some movies with the various film stars that he fancies. He knows the leader of the village council, and although he does not know the prime minister of the country, he knows the present and past chief ministers of the state. While talking to him, he is informed that a film is being shown at Raju Ram's house by Anil. He rushes to see the movie. At Raju Ram's home a VCD is being played and around ten to fifteen kids are present. At about 1930 the movie ends and when the TV is switched off, Ashok and the others leave for home.

Ashok is a sentimental and disciplined child. He is interested in his studies and does his work happily. Sometimes he watches TV; when asked to go to school he goes there; when asked to cut grass he does so. He never asks his parents to buy anything when a vendor comes to the village. He is well aware of his family's financial situation.

Pinki Kumari has a different kind of character. She is less obedient and enjoys adventure and freedom in which she compares herself favourably with the girls of upper castes who lead a more restricted life. Pinki is a thirteen-year-old girl of the lower Chamar caste and lives in a nearby village in Bihar. Her father is illiterate, but her mother studied up to the sixth class. She has an elder brother, an elder sister, and two younger brothers. The family lives in a bamboo house. Her father Aklu Ram is an attached labourer in a Bhumihar household, where her mother also works. Aklu Ram had borrowed a sum of Rs. 5.000 (100 euro), at a 5% monthly interest rate, to marry off his daughter. In order to get the money needed to repay the debt, the eldest son decided to migrate to Punjab in search of work. His remittances have brought some comfort to the household. The father seems quite indifferent towards Pinki's education. However, the mother wants Pinki to attend school. Pinki herself has thought about her future and envisages a life in which she will be enterprising and earn enough money for the necessary luxuries which she expects to have.

Box 4.3 A Day in the Life of Pinki

0450   Pinki wakes up and goes into the field to defecate.

0515   Pinki retrieves the sweeping brush from under the bed where she was sleeping and starts sweeping; while her mother is engaged in the kitchen, her father sweeps the inner portion of the house. According to Pinki, she began helping her mother in the kitchen and other household tasks after her elder sister Rinki was married off and left the house. There seems to be a perfect coordination between her and the mother. While working together, they discuss a number of frivolous matters such as forthcoming festivals, the expecting female buffalo, and the debt they incurred for the elder sister's marriage. Both seem concerned about the welfare of the father who is not keeping well.

0600   After her mother has finished washing the utensils, she helps in preparing the *chulha* (earthen oven) for the food. She brings some dry leaves to light the fire. Pinki picks up an iron bucket, goes to the hand pump, fills it up and puts it near her mother who uses the water for washing rice and *dal*.

0715   She then goes for her tuition. Baju, a graduate, teaches a group of disadvantaged village children in the morning. The teacher himself belongs to the same Chamar caste.

0845   Pinki comes back home, takes a bath, washes her clothes and puts them to dry. Her mother has gone out to bring home soil for wall plastering, before going to work for the landlord. Pinki serves her own food: rice, *dal*, and potato curry. She eats and washes the utensils and then goes to school. Her school bag contains a worn-out slate, some torn books, and a pen. Although she has a notebook, she mostly uses the slate.

1000   She reaches school and does her schoolwork. She sits in the second row and often talks to the other children, or leaves the classroom; the teacher does not pay attention. The teacher goes for tea, and the children start playing with stones. When the teacher comes into the class, the game stops. The teacher asks to take out the Hindi book and to read the texts on their own. When the teacher leaves the classroom, which happens a number of times, the children start playing. When she returns, she sets a new excercise without really instructing the children or monitoring their progress.

1330   Pinki comes back home during the break. On the way, she stops for a while at a shop where some people are busy watching TV, and then also wanders around into the garden or fields in order to collect some fruit. Pinki is a fun-loving girl. At school or at home, she does not miss a chance to enjoy herself. She is daring too. She dares to swim even in fast currents and she is not afraid of going into fields and plucking lychees or bananas; in fact she leads the group in these mischievous acts.

1430   Pinki decides not to go back to school after the break as she has to plaster the walls of her house. The mother asks Pinki to mix the soil with water and prepare it for plastering. Pinki sits on the ground and pours some water into the soil and mixes it with both hands. They put the plaster on the wooden frame of their house, and then smooth it out.

1630   Pinki's mother has cut grass for the buffalo and brings it home. Pinki beats it to clean it.

(continued)

Box 4.3 A Day in the Life of Pinki *(continued)*

1720	Helped by her mother, she cuts the grass into tiny pieces to feed the buffalo. Her mother inserts the grass into the cutting machine while Pinki rotates the knife with the handle.
1800	Her brother brings a sugarcane stick from somewhere. She likes the sugarcane, and they compete with each other as to who can eat a greater portion of the sugarcane in one bite.
1825	She goes to Shyam's house to study. Raghu Ram, a middle-aged school teacher, calls the schoolchildren to his house and makes them sit to study and do their homework. They sit on the wooden bench with a lantern in the middle. Pinki says that she goes to school because she would like to work in a children's centre one day and help the villagers in many ways.
1940	She comes back home, and eats her evening meal *(roti)*.
2000	Prepares her bed and goes to sleep.

Pinki goes to school, but school does not seem to be the priority. During the second day of observation Pinki decides not to go to school at all since so much work has to be done at home. The work at home, the tuition, and the freedom to hop around are the three aspects that structure her days. Since school is unattractive for the way children are being treated and knowledge is (not) transferred, Pinki, who is eager to learn, does not see school as a priority. She again wakes up at 4:50 a.m., that early because women have to relieve themselves in the fields when it is still dark. Pinki loathes this public exposure. Her mother wants her to finish the wall plastering, and takes Pinki along with her to collect the soil. While the mother does the digging, Pinki makes four trips to the house with the heavy wooden basket on her head. While her mother is later preparing the vegetables, she asks Pinki to prepare the *masala*, a job which Pinki dislikes since the grinding stone is very heavy. Pinki then takes the food to her father. While returning from the field where her father works, she stops to watch TV at Raju's house for about ten minutes. She likes to watch TV. She knows the actors and actresses; Karishma Kapoor is her favourite heroine and Govinda her favourite hero. She regrets that she cannot watch as much TV as she wants. She returns home where she finds her mother still doing the walls, and starts to help. Then a woman from the neighbourhood comes to ask Pinki to read a letter for her. Pinki reads the letter correctly, although with quite some difficulty because she finds the handwriting very untidy. After they finish their food, there is a call for her mother from the landlords' house. Her mother asks Pinki to give the plaster a finishing touch and fetch some dry leaves for cooking.

Pinki understands that she is poor, and dislikes it, but she feels that she has more freedom and fun opportunities than her upper-caste Bhumihar counterparts, as they cannot run in the fields freely or go swimming or collect fruit in the gardens. Pinki can think of many ways to achieve her wishes. She is fashionable too, as she uses shampoo in her hair. She says that she wants to wear nice dresses, but she cannot afford to buy any. She wants to make it into the modern world and would like to go to town and do some shopping. She hopes to earn good money through the sale of her handmade bamboo baskets. However, she has the disposition of the adults against her. When Pinki's father was asked about sending Pinki to a local training centre, he said that it would only add to the financial burden:

> A girl is a burden in itself. Teaching her or giving her opportunities will not render any benefit as she has to be married off very soon anyway and then she will work or earn for that family. So what is the use of teaching a girl? A girl is useful doing the household jobs. A girl should only know how to write and read letters.

4.4. CHILDREN IN THE INDIAN CITIES: THREE CASES

Conditions of children in the city, even in poor neighbourhoods like the slum areas of Dar es Salaam, New Delhi, and La Paz, are different from the lives of children in the countryside. They usually have ready access to a TV, and that takes up a lot of their leisure time, leaving them little time to roam around and play. They, however, usually also go to school, and since the schools exert more discipline than many schools in the countryside, attendance is usually high. Below are three cases from the slums around New Delhi.

In Govindpuri (New Delhi) the daily activities of children are perceptibly different from those observed in the villages. The talk of the children is even different (film and cricket stars are a hot item), their dances and songs are different (taken directly from the film world rather than the traditional folk dances and music), and their spending pattern is different. The children relish ice cream, biscuits, chocolates, etc., even if only a few times a week. Some girls said that their parents give them pocket money regularly and thus they manage to eat their favourite things, and also save some to buy fancy items like nail polish, ornaments, etc. In the cities, we generally find children who have moved closer to the standard perception of a Western childhood with comparable lifestyles.

Practically all the younger children go to school. They know that it is necessary and they like it. Most teachers treat them well, although some of them tend to lose their temper and scold the pupils. Most complaints by the children from the poor, lower-caste neighbourhoods which we studied, are about female teachers, who usually come from higher castes and are living in respectable neighbourhoods. They tend to use derogatory language such as, 'you slum dwellers, you smell bad', 'keep away from me, you are smelling bad', 'you don't need to study, go and work like your mother as house maid', 'you are useless', and so forth. The psychological violence which many of the children have to undergo reinforces the feeling of downtrodden slum dwellers without a proper place in society. The school which ideally should act as an institution of equivalence actually then reinforces the class divisions of society at large.

Jaimala, a thirteen-year-old girl, studies in class seven of a Hindi medium school near her house in Govindpuri. The family, with two boys and one daughter, migrated from Agra in 1980. The father is not working; he spends his money on gambling. The mother works on daily wages and the in-laws run a small shop and make envelopes. Suriti, a niece from Agra, lives with

---

Box 4.4 A Day in the Life of Jaimala, a Sunday

0800 The father is still sleeping and the mother has already gone to work. The younger brother is playing in the street. Jaimala wakes up and tells me that she usually wakes up around 6:30 but since it is a holiday, she has slept late. She goes upstairs to brush her teeth and have a bath.

0900 They have a single room attached to a small shop opening onto the street. Inside the room there is a gas stove placed on the cupboard. Jaimala starts making *chappati* and tea and all the family members have their breakfast. After breakfast, Jaimala and Suriti clean the utensils.

1000 There is a small space in between the room and the entrance of the house. Grandmother sits down there and starts her work. Jaimala's grandfather is cutting paper to make *lifafa*. Jaimala and Suriti join the grandmother in folding and gluing the envelopes. After making one hundred *lifafa* of different sizes Jaimala takes the *lifafa* upstairs and spreads them out to dry.

1200 Grandmother asks for the vegetable basket and starts chopping the vegetables. Jaimala cooks lentils and fries the vegetables. Jaimala warms the *chappati* which she made for breakfast and all of them including Yogendra, who has been playing outside, have lunch. Before they finish their lunch, the father comes home and joins them.

1300 After lunch Suriti takes the utensils upstairs and Jaimala follows her with a bucket of water. Jaimala comes down and cleans the place where they had lunch and helps Suriti with the utensils and puts them in the cupboard.

1400 An irregular water tap next door is used to fetch drinking water. The auntie next door calls out for Jaimala that water is coming. Her grandmother takes two jerry cans and fills them with water. Jaimala and Suriti carry them over to the kitchen.

1500 Mattresses are spread out in the room shared by Jaimala, Suriti, and the grandmother. Jaimala and Suriti lie down and sleep.

1600 Jaimala's grandmother makes tea and wakes up Suriti and Jaimala. They wash their faces and have a cup of tea. Jaimala then collects the *lifafa*. Then Jaimala and Suriti put them in boxes.

1700 The neighbour next door has only one son who is working and so she is alone most of the time. They go to her place to watch TV. Jaimala and Suriti watch a serial and come back home.

1800 Jaimala and Suriti take out their school bags and do their homework. They work until 1930 when they have dinner and then go to bed.

them. Jaimala is the middle child; she pays a monthly school fee of Rs. 100/-, of which she is given Rs. 50/- in return, as a reward for regular attendance and homework completion. In her free time she makes *lifafa* (envelopes). The eldest son is blind and studies in a special school. Yogendra is the youngest son studying in the fourth standard; he is ten years old.

Jaimala, with some time in between for watching television at a neighbour's house and having a siesta in the afternoon, on her school-free Sunday is engaged in household chores, substituting for her mother, and envelope making for the better part of the day. Manoj's family is slightly better off, even though the living conditions appear to be worse. They live with seven people (father, mother, and five children) in a small single-roomed house,

---

Box 4.5 A Day in the Life of Manoj

0700	The public toilet is located at some five meters distance. It is extremely unclean. After coming from the toilet she washes her legs and hands with water.
0730	The water pipe is just adjacent to the house. Manoj fetches eight to ten cans of water. Her elder sister assists her in bringing the water to the house. Since her mother is pregnant, she does not do any heavy work. There is a big queue to fetch water and an argument breaks out over who came first and who consumes more water.
1000	Manoj has three *roti* with *subji* (vegetable curry, prepared by her sister) and half a glass of tea as breakfast. She feeds her younger sister.
1030	She watches TV for half an hour, without much interest.
1100	She starts doing her homework (Maths & English). She has a blunt pencil and an eraser. Around midday her younger sister takes away the eraser, refuses to give it back and goes out into the street. Manoj follows her to take back the eraser but gets herself involved in the game.
1300	She eats four *roti*, *subji*, and rice. The food was prepared in the morning. She washes the plates.
1330	While watching a Hindi movie, she falls asleep and then gets up at around 1630.
1630	She goes to buy milk and then goes out to meet her friends. There are no playing areas nearby, but in her aunt's house there is a little space where they can chat.
1730	She wants to make tea, but the kerosene in the stove is finished and she has to go to the shop again to buy it. After drinking tea, she cleans all the glasses.
1830	She asks permission of her mother to visit the temple nearby. With her brother, she stays in the temple for five minutes, and then comes out and stands in the line for *prasad*. Both are given *prasad* on a small disposable plate, which she brings home.
1900	After returning from the temple, she shares her *prasad* with all people at home. Her sister prepares dinner: *chappati* and *subji*.
1945	Everybody sits on the floor for food. The eldest daughter serves the food.

roofed with asbestos sheets and surrounded by an open sewer drain. In one corner of the room there is a table holding a kerosene stove and provisions. In another corner there is a small sink with an outlet connected to the street's drainage system; this space is used for cleaning utensils, washing clothes, bathing, and sometimes to attend to the call of nature. There is also one cot and a black-and-white portable TV. Father is a carpenter who migrated from a village in Northern India some ten years back and the mother undertakes embroidery work on piece–rate basis as and when available. The elder sister, Saroj (eleven) carries out a major portion of the household chores. Manoj is ten and studies in class four. The three younger children are also in school. Below is a day out of the life of Manoj. This day also is a holiday.

Both the cases above, describing the daily activities of two girls on a Sunday, show considerable involvement in household activities. Although most of the children were going to school and were not found participating in wage employment, almost all the children in the two Delhi slums were found to be involved in household activities in varying intensity. Urban slum life with poor basic civic amenties, low incomes, and a low productive nature of work lead to the involvement of children in adult chores and responsibilities. Although girls are found to devote more time on unpaid household activities and boys usually spend more time with wage work, the division was not as obvious as feminist theory would suggest. Below are two cases of activities during a school day. Phool Jaha is the thirteen-year-old daughter of Ali Mohamad, a labourer, and Ayesha, who runs a shop adjoining the house. They migrated to Delhi twenty years ago, and now live in Pritampura. She has four younger brothers. The two younger brothers do not attend school yet. Phool Jaha is in the sixth class of a government school. She studies well but in the end, at home, spends more time in doing household chores than in studying. At the age of thirteen, she has learned to take full responsibility for the running of the household in the absence of her mother.

Jaybeer, a boy in another Delhi slum, is the eldest son in the family, which migrated some five years ago from a village in nearby Haryana. In this case also, the parents are busy in earning money and Jaybeer, in addition to going to school, takes on a big responsibility in the small shop which his father is running just a few doors from their house. Jaybeer's mother is a housewife, but there is a flour mill at his home, which is used to grind flour for local people. He has two sisters and one brother. Two of Jaybeer's aunts live nearby, which results in all the cousins being at his house most of the time. The family lives in a single-roomed house. The house has a double cot, a refrigerator, a colour (portable) TV, and a flour machine, all crammed into one small room.

Jaybeer leaves for school soon after seven in the morning and returns home at 1330. He changes his uniform and sits down for lunch. Afterwards, he goes to the shop so that his father can go home for lunch. He manages

Box 4.6 A Day in the Life of Phool Jaha

0715   When I reach the house, Phool Jaha is waiting for me. We reach the school before the school bell rings exactly at 0730. The pupils assemble in lines, sing and pray and then go to their respective classes.

0745   The classroom does not have any windows; it just has a ventilator on the ceiling. The science class (in Hindi) is followed with rapt attention. The maths teacher, who comes next, explains a problem and asks the students to solve it; most students fail to do so, and after the teacher explains, she give them another problem to solve as homework. Then comes the Sanskrit teacher. None of the students pay attention to the teacher who scolds them repeatedly. They are more interested in what the next teacher, social studies, explains. Phool Jaha attends the class attentively. The teacher asks the students to read the chapter and then asks them related questions.

1100   Some of the children have brought their lunch boxes, so they sit and eat; others are playing. Phool Jaha joins me during the break and with her friends we roam around the playground.

1200   The English teacher has not turned up and the pupils go out to the playground. They form groups of two or three and start chatting.

1300   The road is crowded with students returning home. Talking to her classmates, we reach home in fifteen minutes. She changes her school uniform and then she takes out a bucket filled with clothes that has been soaked by her mother earlier; she goes to the pump where she does the washing, has a bath, and changes into clean clothes.

1400   A lunch of *dal*, *subji*, and rice. She cleans the room and has lunch; in the meantime, her younger brothers come back from school and join her for lunch. She then cleans the utensils and mops the room.

1500   The children soon fall asleep on the bed.

1615   After waking up, they wash their faces. Spreading the rug on the floor, she sits down to study. She solves her maths problems and helps her brother with his homework.

1730   After completing her homework, she goes to her mother's shop to help her out. Thereafter, when the mother goes inside, Phool Jaha closes the shop.

1815   All the family members except the father sit down on the rug and watch TV. Phool Jaha also helps her mother in the kitchen work.

1930   After dinner, they immediately go and sleep.

the shop pretty well, weighing the goods and calculating the prices. By 1500 he is back home and watches cartoons and then he sleeps for an hour. He is woken up by his mother at around 1700 and told to go and assist his father. Jaybeer is given Rs. 500 to go and buy new supplies (cigarettes, pan, chocolates, sugar) at the wholesale shop. He comes back with a big bag, and then assists his father. Since there are more customers now, Jaybeer handles the goods and his father handles the money. He returns home by 1830 to do some homework and to have dinner.

CONCLUSION

Leisure time is a hybrid concept and appears to be very much related to local opportunities. Whereas leisure time in developed countries involves participation in sports, playing grounds, computer games, internet and television, for poor children in developing countries, none of these, with the exception recently of television, exist. Playing around with friends and, in the cities, watching television are comparable to the activities which children in the developed countries undertake. But most of the time which children were engaged in outside school hours was actually spent on working. Such work was not exactly labour though. It was time applied to doing the things that were needed for the upkeep of the house and the family. It involved such activities as looking after younger children, sweeping the house, fetching water, cleaning the utensils, repairing the house, etc. It intertwined with playing and socialising.

Whereas there is a debate whether a distinction should be made between child labour and child work (see Chapter 6), there also could be a debate on work and leisure. Hauling water from a deep well and carrying big pots of water over a long distance, as we noticed in one of the examples, may indeed not be qualified as leisure, but much else what the children were doing was felt as an enjoyable pastime, particularly since it often went hand in hand with playing and chatting. Practically all the children were spending at least two hours on household chores and, under the internationally accepted norms, would thus qualify to be included as child labourers. Such norms, however, are not readily applicable since leisure and light forms of work cannot be separated.

The activities of the children are integral to the process of socialisation and often increase the self-esteem of the child. This positive attitude is one of solidarity and responsibility and reflects the place of the child within a family structure. For most of these children, the family home is a place where they find love and protection. Luckily for the child, that was the case in most families. It was not in the exceptional case, where the child was ill-treated, the family was steeped in poverty and was torn apart by dysfunctional behaviour of one of the parents, usually the alcoholic father. It is difficult to relate the discussion which some academics, particularly economists, have on the so-called egoistic and altruistic parents to the field reality. It was generally difficult to qualify parents as being driven by egoistic notions in relation to their children, exploiting them for their private end. Parents, because of their own cultural background, may in many cases not have insisted more vehemently on the child going to school and they may not have provided the child with more leisure time. The best interest of the child, however, usually was central to their concern.

Boys are more involved in labour, and are directly in interaction with the market. Girls are trained by their mothers, from a very young age, to clean the house, manage the kitchen, prepare tea, cook and serve food, wash clothes, serve guests, care for younger siblings, and so forth. However, in a few case studies in Andhra and Bihar, in Vietnam, Nicaragua, and Bolivia, boys were also documented to be washing clothes, cleaning utensils, and looking after younger siblings. On the other hand boys, more so than girls, are generally expected to collect provisions from the shops, accompany a younger brother or sister to school, fetch water form the pump, go to the market, and so on. In terms of leisure activities, there too seems to be a gender division, although some activities overlap. Boys were documented playing cricket, playing cards, going to the movies. Girls are more likely to be seen roaming around, talking to friends or mixing work/ school with pleasure.

5   School and Education

There is an increasing acknowledgment that education is a fundamental right and that governments must ensure that universal primary education is achieved by 2015. Educational conditions varied between the countries involved in this study. Particularly Vietnam appears to have been successful in its primary school enrolment, and it even shows high levels of attendance in the secondary school system. Some other countries, however, particularly Burkina Faso, still present bleak statistics. Differences within countries are also significant. In India, for example, the near perfect enrolment rates of the urban primary schools contrast sharply with those of the rural areas in the less developed states. Individual schools can be attractive, or unattractive, for many reasons. In this chapter, reasons for attending school or not will be explored.

5.1. ATTENDANCE AND SCHOOL FACILITIES

One of the factors influencing school attendance appears to be the condition of the school facilities. In Nicaragua, attendance was remarkably high. We calculated that in the six to seventeen age group of the 490 children in our sample, school attendance was as high as 85%. In Vietnam attendance in the same age group was even higher. Most of the schools in Nicaragua were in good condition; they had spacious classrooms with educationally decorated walls, and some even had a library. Schools in Vietnam are generally well built and well equipped; the high teacher–pupil ratio (around thirty pupils in a class) stimulates an inviting environment for the children. The accessibility of schools is a precondition to a good education. Even in Vietnam, as schools and classrooms are in short supply in many communities, the children have to hustle into narrow classrooms, with poor light and sanitation conditions. In some locations in Vietnam, the pupils have to learn in three 'shifts' a day, and have to sit in classrooms which although poorly equipped are tidy and comfortable.

The well-furnished and neatly maintained schools are possibly not directly the reason why children like to attend them. They are a reflection of the commitment of the authorities and of the teachers to provide a child-friendly environment. The paucity of resources available to the school management was only part of the reason why in other countries, school buildings were dilapidated and dirty: children were supposed to sit and learn in an environment in which neither the buildings nor the staff were accommodative. In Nicaragua and Vietnam, however, schools provided a proper surrounding and children felt that they were welcome and looked after properly. It was a place which in terms of material conditions in any case was not worse than home.

In Bolivia, however, respectively 35% and 27% of the children in Santa Cruz and El Torno stated that they were seriously dissatisfied with their school's facilities (Moreno 2002, 99 and 161). Julio (fourteen), attending the day school in El Torno, explained, 'The biggest problem we have here is that our whole school is in a bad state actually. The windows are shattered, the paint comes off the walls, the seats are broken, and the doors and school boards are also broken'. Some of the problems with the facilities are aggravated by circumstances prevailing in the area. For example, of all the schools in Bolivia that we studied, all but one had broken windows. However, this problem had particular implications in El Alto, especially for the evening schools, because of the cold weather prevailing there for much of the year. Maikel (thirteen), who attends the evening school in El Alto, complained about the windows and the cold: 'One can hardly keep sitting with this cold, one can hardly write. Your hands will be freezing. Therefore we have to sit here with our coats, hats, and gloves on'. If the winter turns extremely cold, classes are cancelled altogether. The poor conditions in the schools negatively affect the level of education that the children attending the public schools receive, especially in comparison with children who attend private schools, which have heating.

The common lack of clean water in many Bolivian schools has drastic consequences for hygiene. The thirteen-year-old Elvira, of the day school in Cochabamba, explained: 'One of the biggest problems here is the situation of our bathrooms. There is no water, and you just cannot go in because of the smell. Everything just stays there if you understand what I mean'. The frequent absence of illumination on the school playgrounds has serious consequences for the safety in some of the evening schools. Edgar, who is eleven and attends the evening school in El Alto, explained how schools, which should be places of protection and safety, can in fact be treacherous areas: 'There are a lot of youth gangs here in El Alto. Because we have no lights on our playground, they come here and sit in the playground. They just group around in the dark corners, and so it is dangerous to go outside during the break'. During the study, we witnessed three gang-related fights in El Alto, one involving a boy of fourteen who was stabbed and taken to hospital.

The problems with inadequate facilities were evident in most schools in the study, but especially those in the rural areas of Burkina Faso, Tanzania,

India, and in the state-run schools in Bolivia. There are holes in the walls and roofs are leaking, children sit on the ground or on bricks, the toilets are often just a hole in the ground, there is no clean water, and so on. However, although the material conditions of the schools do make school attendance less attractive, the value of education in general is by and large not in doubt. Practically all parents told us that education helps children to prepare for a better future; it develops their talents and it increases job opportunities. But such preparation is a strenuous affair if children have to sit in cramped rooms, without much ventilation in the stagnant summer heat, or broken windows in the biting cold, or with only a worn-out blackboard as an educational support tool. The dilapidated conditions often are a reflection of the disinterest which teachers have for their profession and for the child and such disinterest evokes a disinterest for schools in the child.

The expansion of the educational system, en route to universal enrolment which the world is supposed to achieve by 2015, has attracted many children from poor and even destitute families. The construction of new school buildings, closer to the habitat of the poor communities, has drawn more children, particularly girls, into the educational system. If children have to travel long distances to reach their schools, that time is considered better spent contributing to household chores or to just playing around. The gender differences can indeed be overcome by targeted interventions by the government, in some cases aided by voluntary agencies. A comparison of school participation in two villages in Rajasthan in India is illustrative of this. In the two villages, overall literacy used to be at remarkably low levels and the discrepancy between male and female literacy was huge. In the village Paltan, 56% of the males and only 20% of the females used to be literate; in the village Kotri, the levels were 53% and 30% respectively. Public intervention for the promotion of literacy, implemented in Kotri, drastically changed the literacy levels. Whereas percentages of literacy in Paltan went up to 88.6% for boys and 38.1% for girls, Kotri saw an impressive rise to 94.6% for boys and 78.3% for girls. The improvement in literacy, especially of girls, appears to have been the result of the erection of a number of schools in Kotri. More importantly, access to these institutions by the girls and boys of poor families was made easy, as they are located in the areas where they live. Whereas in earlier days, they belonged to the marginalised sections, at the margin of the educational system, now they had become at the centre of attention. They lived up to the expectations.

The case study of Rajasthan reveals that when schools and advocacy programmes are brought into poorer neighbourhoods, the impact can be remarkable. The night school initiated by an NGO has provided a crucial space for girls to attend school after completing their daily household chores. Heera is an excellent example of this.

Heera (fourteen) is the eldest of five daughters in a low-caste and landless Bagaria household in Patan, a semidesert village in Rajasthan. The father works, mostly at distant places, as a construction labourer or in the

---

Box 5.1 A Day in the Life of Heera

0600　Heera gets up at 6 a.m., as usual. After washing her face and brushing her teeth, together with two of her cousins, she leaves for the well, which is half a kilometre away. She carries a rubber rope, a bucket and two pitchers, one of fifteen litres on her head and the other of five litres on the hips. The well is nearly eighty feet deep. She draws a bucketful of water at least four times, and then stops, gasping for breath. After filling the pitchers, she lifts them to her head, with the help of her cousins, and carries them home. She fills a small cement tank with water, and then returns to the well for a second round. Then she sweeps the room and the veranda with a broom made of small twigs. She also cleans the open shed where the goats and the heifer were tied at night.

0800　Heera has her breakfast of one and half *bajra roti* (flat grain cakes) with *chhach* (curd mixed with water). Her mother has prepared the *roti*. The *chhach* was given to her yesterday when she went to clean the courtyard of a neighbour, as she does on alternate days. She takes her bath at the back of the house, puts on new clothes, and washes her clothes. She sweeps the courtyard, puts the dirt in a pot and throws the dirt away. She finishes the job by 0945 and then stands under the veranda for fifteen minutes.

1000　She asks her cousins Mandor and Gita to accompany her bringing water since, after everybody had his bath, the water is finished. She walks to the well, draws the water, fills the pitchers and reaches home by 1040.

1045　She talks with her cousins about their night school teacher and the breakfast they had in the morning. Her mother Sugni Devi asks her to take care of her youngest sister Niraj while she prepares to go out with Niraj to go and see the doctor. Heera's younger sister Bidan (ten) has taken the sheep to graze. At 1115, Heera is alone with the two younger sisters, and with her cousin Gita. They talk about various subjects while keeping an eye on the younger sisters.

1330　The family has lunch and then they lie down and sleep.

1500　Her cousin Gita joins her. Heera and Gita bring their books. They do some drawings. They joke with each other while seeing the picture of the animals in the book. Heera's mother calls her to attend to her youngest sister Niraj. Heera takes Niraj and washes her.

1545　Heera, along with her cousins Mandor and Gita, goes and fetches water from a nearby well (three hundred metres), which has hard water that will be used for washing clothes and taking baths. After they have hauled the bucket four times and the pitchers have been filled, these are carried home.

1600　Bidan, Heera's sister, has returned with the two goats and the heifer. Heera ties the goats and the heifer with a rope. She brings firewood and breaks it into small pieces. Then she sweeps the kitchen/veranda, lights the kitchen fire, kneads flour, and prepares *roti* and *dal*.

1830　All the children of the house eat dinner. Heera cleans the dishes after dinner.

1900　After dinner she rests for a while. Her cousins Gita and Mandor join her. They prepare for school. The school is right in front of her house. She takes two books and a slate with her.

(continued)

Box 5.1 A Day in the Life of Heera *(continued)*

1915	Mr. Mustaq, the teacher, is on time and a few minutes after the children arrive, lessons start. Heera recites multiplication tables and does some drawings on her slate. She sits with her cousin Mandor. They often laugh and jostle each other. Heera returns home at around 2130.
2145	After returning from school she talks for a while with her cousins before she spreads a quilt on the cot and lies down to rest. The cot is in the courtyard under the open sky. Her younger sisters have already fallen asleep. Her mother sleeps on the veranda with the youngest daughter Niraj by her side. Her father sleeps on another cot.

saltpans. He comes home for a couple of days every fortnight. The mother mostly stays in the home, but on some days, she goes out to work as a daily labourer. She has three other small children to attend to: Rekha (four), Sita (three), and Niraj (one). Heera, unlike many of the girls of her age, is still unmarried. She attends the night school run by a local NGO. She has her small desires, like Coca-Cola or apples, or sweets and bananas, which her father brings from town a couple of times each month. She dreams of a sewing machine and of television, which she has watched only a few times. We observed her on three consecutive days in October 2002. Below is an exact notation of one day, followed by summaries of the next two days. She has a busy programme looking after the household, tending to a younger sister, and collecting water from different wells. In the evening, after a hard day's work, she can spend two hours in school.

On the first day, Heera spends five hours and fifteen minutes on household work, not including the time spent on looking after the baby, and only two hours and thirty minutes on school and studying. The second day is fairly similar. Heera gets up at six o'clock, folds her quilt, washes her face, and brushes her teeth. She fetches water from the well, and then has breakfast (*bajra roti* and chilli paste) prepared by her mother in the morning. At 0830, she prepares to go to the jungle, with her cousins and a girl from the neighbourhood, to fetch firewood. All of them have an axe and a rope. They walk at least four kilometres, and then start cutting the small trees. After about an hour, they tie brushwood, around 20 kg, into a bundle. After a rest, whilst talking about the scorching sun, they begin their homeward journey. She walks home with the load of firewood on her head and the axe in her hand. She unloads the firewood near the entrance of the house, and sits for a while on the veranda.

At 1230, Heera has her bath, before having lunch with her sisters. She then lies down and sleeps for more than an hour. At 1500 her mother wakes her, and asks her to fetch water with Gita and Mandor. They make two round trips to the well. After returning home they rest and talk with each other for half an hour. Heera then sweeps the courtyard. Then again they talk, until around 6 p.m. Today is *Navratra*, a festival observed by all the households of the village. They talk about the special dishes that will be prepared today and they discuss among themselves how to prepare these dishes and to make them tasty. The special dinner today, which will take longer to prepare than normal, consists of a mixture of rice and lentils (*kichri*), deep-fried *roti* and lentils. At around 1900 they have dinner, for which Gita and Mandor have brought the food prepared at home. Afterwards Heera, Gita, and Mandor wash the dishes. They joke and laugh a lot. At 2030, the mother tells Heera to go to bed. She takes her quilt, spreads it on the cot and goes to sleep after washing her legs, arms, and face.

Day three is similar to the second day, except for the visit to the village shop around noon, where both Mandor and Heera buy two bottles of nail polish, and the night school, which lasts for only one hour since the teacher arrives late. Heera dislikes the teacher being late, because, as she says, illiteracy is poverty: 'An illiterate is more often a poor man than a literate. A poor man has no source of income.' The lessons at the evening school have made her literate and have taught her some knowledge of mathematics. Classes last for less than two hours and Heera wants to utilise that time to the brim.

The improvement in school facilities, the accessibility of schools, and the sustained campaigns around education, are unmistakably essential to the achievement of universal primary education. Villages with poorly maintained schools experience high levels of 'out of school children'. The schools in both the villages which we studied in Burkina Faso suffered from an acute lack of facilities and teachers. The government had expanded the school infrastructure in the 1980s, constructing school buildings in remote areas, but the new political regime and economic policy in the 1990s has shifted the priorities, and many schools were left without operating expenses or even teachers. NGOs, like PLAN International, moved in to close the gap. One village elder told us: 'Ouagadougou told us to go and look for friends abroad if we wanted to pay our teachers'. There is only one primary school in Dem for both girls and boys, and only about one-third of the children are in school. The rest have never gone to school or have dropped out. The school is too far away for most children, and it is of poor quality anyway. Classes are often cancelled and so children start preferring to help out at home instead. In Dem we encountered an extended household with twenty-three children not attending school and three going to school; in another household six children were in school and four children were not attending school. Decisions about going to school were apparently based on the personal inclination of the child. School was a place which one could go to if one liked but since it did not have much to offer, many children either never went or dropped out. In Batie the situation was comparatively better, with three primary schools and one high school. The higher level of participation (around two-thirds of the children) may be attributable to the relative awareness of the value of education but also to the better material conditions of the school infrastructure. The material conditions of the school building reflected a more conscious role of the teacher and this possibly had its impact on the participation of the children.

5.2. ATTENDANCE AND POVERTY

A second factor that influences school attendance is the occurrence of child labour. The need to work appears to be a reason for some children not to attend school, although often attendance and work are combined. Although the large majority of the people we spoke to regarded school as instrumental in contributing to the personal development of the child, most of these people were critical about how education would affect the future chances for employment.

Even if children do attend school, they may still spend quite a lot of time working after school hours. Mr. Vu Dinh C., the principal of La Son lower secondary school in Vietnam, commented: 'Many of my students go to school in the morning, and in the afternoon they have to catch crabs and shellfish from the field for sale. As a result, they have very little time to learn or do home exercises.' Many of these children indeed have less time for their homework, or even miss classes because they have to work. In the rural areas, the agricultural cycle forms an additional problem since in the labour-intensive seasons all hands are required and on such days children tend to be withdrawn from school. In the harvesting and sowing seasons agricultural activities increase and many children miss classes while working on the family plots. Jessica (ten) attends the morning school in El Torno, Bolivia: 'I do not like missing classes, but during the harvesting and sowing seasons I have to help my family on the land. This makes me miss classes around fifteen times a year'. Julietta (fourteen): 'my mother and father have to work constantly to get some money to eat. In the meanwhile, who has to look after my younger brothers and sister? Me. So that's why I come to school in the evening, and that's why I sometimes miss classes.'

The worst cases of not attending because of work were seen in Burkina Faso, in some states in Tanzania and India, and in Bolivia. It became clear that it is extremely difficult to categorise children as either 'going to school' or 'not going to school'. More common are children who go to school whenever they are not needed elsewhere to work.

By and large, it is not a lack of interest in education that keeps children at home. Children both in urban and rural areas realise the importance of education, but often accept the inability because of their families' economic condition and their responsibility to supplement the family income. Most of the case studies inform us that the value of education is recognised but that actual attendance is dependent on the environment, particularly on the socioeconomic situation of the family. Cases from our study in Tanzania illustrate this point.

In Ifakara, a group of three boys told us that ordinarily they would only help their parents on the farm and with household jobs after school and during the weekend. However, 'when we are in urgent need of money we have to drop classes in order to earn some money, mainly when we need to buy exercise books and pens or in case of emergencies if our parents don't have money'. A girl in Ifakara, the fourteen-year-old Mwajuma, told us that she had finished primary school two years ago and had successfully passed her exams. She was selected for secondary school but she was not able to continue with her education. Her family had saved money to pay for her secondary school fee, but just after her final exams, her mother, elder brother, and sister-in-law got involved in a serious car accident. The money had to be used for medical treatments.

We came across several children in all research locations who, like Mwajuma, had finished primary school but whose parents could not afford to send them to secondary school. Unlike Mwajuma, most of these children had always known that the chance of getting into secondary education was slim, due to the financial situation of their parents. After finishing primary school, these children stayed at home to help their parents with farming and/or small business on a full-time basis, or they just stay at home doing nothing, as a girl told us in Dar es Salaam: 'I don't do anything. I'm waiting for my father until he has saved enough money. It happens often; normally I have to wait for about one month. We didn't meet the deadline for payment, so I had to leave school'. Another girl said that she had never been to school and that she was not expecting to go either. In the period that the Tanzanian government had decided that education should be paid for by the parents, her father did not have the money. When the policy changed and education became free again, she was too old: 'I did ask my father if I could go and he told me that I could go next month. But a month later he told me the same thing and again and again. Later, my mother took me to school for registration, but there they said that I couldn't start because I was too old to enter the first standard.' Another boy in the same area said: 'I cried a lot when I heard that my relatives had an accident. My father had to spend all the money on medical expenses. We sell milk and we don't earn much, less than two thousand shillings per day. So now I have no means, the only option is to stay at home and do some household jobs'.

Not only the children, but also their parents explained that economic constraints at the family level often reduce attendance in school. An example is Felix, the father of Edgar (eleven) in El Alto, Bolivia. The boy works in a *chaperia* (garage), scrubbing the paint off cars that need to be refurbished. He works more than nine hours a day, from 0800 to 1700 with half an hour break at 1300. From 1900 to 2200 he goes to the evening school in El Alto, but sometimes he works late and misses school. Felix would prefer Edgar not to be working but he argues that economic necessity leaves him no other choice:

How much I want my son to study during the day and only having to do his homework, so that he will become a professional and will not suffer like me. But my children also see that we do not have any money, so they go and work and therefore sometimes miss school. But what can we do? Of which money will we eat?

Another example is Adolfo who lives in Cochabamba with five children of whom three are working: David (eleven), Elvis (fourteen), and Wilmer (fifteen). They all attend evening school. Adolfo would prefer his children to be studying instead of working, but he realises that the main problem is that 'we all have to work. I really do not like it that my children work, but where else can I get the money to buy clothes and food. If there were any stable jobs, things perhaps would be better. But since there are none, we have to go on like we do.' An example from the rural city of El Torno in Bolivia is Emmy, the mother of Jherson (thirteen), who attends the evening school. In the sowing and harvesting seasons Jherson is sent to work on the family land. The remaining part of the year, he is active collecting stones from the river for the cement factory in the city. Emmy complains: 'There is no work and we do not earn as much as we used to from our land. With what I earn I cannot provide for my family. That is why my children have to help me, working on the land and help me sell the products in the market.' She recognises that this has negative consequences for the education of her son: 'In the sowing and harvesting seasons we all have to work hard. Therefore we often come late from our land and Jherson is late for school. But what can we do? We have to work with all the family members because, otherwise we will be late with harvesting and this will ruin our crop. And we cannot pay helpers.'

A question that crops up regularly is whether poverty is the crucial factor that prevents children from going to school. School fees in any case make a difference. A fee is often to be paid for more than one child and involves a cash flow, which means that the parents first have to earn the money before they can spend it. In many rural areas, where commoditisation of the economy is still in its infancy and where many families are living in utter deprivation anyway, liquidity as such is the basic problem. When attending school is free, it still implies that the family has to forego the income of the children. In some cases, the opportunity cost could be forbidding, for example when the family depends solely on the income of the child. In other cases, the necessity for the child is not apparent, as in the case of Jherson above. His mother knows that his work has a negative effect on education but she makes him work because she 'cannot pay helpers'. In her 'rational choice', she has weighed the two options and has decided that the boy has to work on the family farm. Such choices appear to be based on rational considerations, but subjective elements do matter, even so much so that parents in the literature are often being blamed for succumbing to short-term egoistic options.

One often tends to forget that the expenditure on education makes up a large percentage of total spending in some households. Primary education in many countries is nominally free, but when the child enters lower secondary school level, parents have to pay various school fees and monthly fees for tutorial classes. Many teachers whom we interviewed took the view that it indeed is poverty that prevents many children from coming to school, but particularly in India and Burkina Faso the absence of children from school was regularly attributed to the selfish and ignorant culture of parents.

An attitude of blaming nonparticipation on the selfishness or disinterest of the parents indeed was not uncommon among the middle-class teachers. There is some evidence to support their view but even among those who hold that belief, poverty is also understood as a major hindrance. Indeed, close observation informed us that work participation and nonenrolment by and large was associated with steep poverty. In Vietnam, for example, poverty had forced many children to drop out. As our sample was focussed mainly on poor households, the number of households with school dropouts made up a rather large percentage (23%). Most of the dropouts, it should be added, were aged twelve to sixteen. The regional differences were interesting: contrary to the expectation, 57.1% of the households with out-of-school children were in Ha Nam, a relatively rich district; 35.7% were in Hanoi; and only 7.1% were in the more remote and less developed Thai Nguyen. Most of the dropouts in the richer areas actually belonged to ethnic minority groups, particularly from the seminomadic Hmong, who are among the poorest in the region, and to children of migrant families who recently had moved into the city (Hanoi) and were still living an unsettled life.

It did not appear ethically correct to condemn poor parents and blaming them rather than the poverty for keeping the children away from school. Poverty sometimes is so penetrating and so constraining, even in a cognitive sense, that school is not a realistic option. One striking example is the following remark made by a teacher in the evening school *Mario Guzman Aspiazu* in El Alto, Bolivia. Her words were directed towards a government official who visited the school to introduce a new educational system. She told him:

> Tell me, what's the use of a new schooling system when our students have to sell their backpacks and books to buy something to eat that night? What is the use of a new method of teaching when our students come here and cannot pay attention because they have an empty stomach and because they are too tired after a whole day working? The government should do something about these problems before they come and tell us how to teach better!

The words of the Bolivian teacher implied that whilst poor children may come to school, their performances are negatively affected by their poverty. High numbers of pupils show up for class hungry and tired from a long day of work and a lack of food and rest. It was not uncommon, even in the relatively short time that we observed the children in the evening school, to frequently see them falling asleep in class. They were eager to attend school but were exhausted by the time they reached the classroom.

An additional problem with children who work and study is that they often only start going to school at a later age, and soon end up sitting in classrooms with children who are much younger than they themselves. This results in a sense of shame (*vergüenza*) or *sharam* (India). Being embarrassed due to one's own poverty is a reason for some children to avoid school. One child confided his envy and shame: 'Our parents are not able to buy new clothes for us. During holidays, there are parents buying new clothes for their children. It is embarrassing seeing other children wearing nice clothes while I have to wear old and dirty clothes.' Another child in urban Dar es Salaam explained:

> There are those children coming from rich families and who are upsetting children from poor families. They are the ones who are able to pay for the tuition and be good in their studies. They are smart because they can pay for extra tuition. They also do not want to mix with children coming from poor families. This is because you can easily recognize children who are coming from poor families and those who are coming from rich families. Children from rich families come with a lot of money to school and they do not want us to be around them because they think that we will steal their money.

The overall attitude of parents towards education is that children should go to school. In that sense, education has become a universal aspiration, but due to factors mentioned above, education has yet to become a universal option. Age, gender, the economic status of the family, and the quality and accessibility of the schools can lead to a decision to discontinue schooling. In the case of girls, moral considerations (the anxiety caused by their social vulnerability) and the preparation for married life form an additional hindrance to education.

Poverty and the experience in the job market, as revealed in numerous case studies, makes the investment in secondary schooling, which is expensive and requires travelling, even less an option than primary education. There has been an influential debate among economists on the luxury theorem. Basu and Van (1988) had suggested that all parents have a choice between two options: to invest in the education of the child today (with an opportunity cost: foregoing income today) or to send the child to work and generating income while foregoing a better future. The discussion around this choice seemed to accept the improved chances of a well-paying and steady job as a reward for education as a given. The field reality, however, indicates a different scenario: well-paying jobs are by and large out of reach for the children of poor families, even if they have invested in education.

5.3. ATTENDANCE AND THE QUALITY OF EDUCATION

There is also a problem with the quality and content of the education itself. Schools, particularly in the less developed areas, have simply not been good enough to attract or retain children. Schools tend to dissipate knowledge that is based on the culture and the occupational needs of the middle class rather than on the worldviews, experiences, and aspirations of the children of the poor. The disjoint is more acute in areas where education has not been established as a social norm. In Burkina Faso, for example, some children whom we interviewed in Dem and Batie would rather work than be subjected to a school regime that is considered irrelevant to their needs. Assane (thirteen) said:

> I do not need to go school. What can I learn there? It is not helpful. I know children who went to school. Their parents spent money paying for their schooling. But you see them without work, they are useless to their families and they do not know anything about life.

The villages in Burkina Faso were the furthest from the child rights' discourse common to a 'modernising' society. The concept of a modernising society is used here as a shortcut for a society in which development takes place along a pattern which generally is associated with such values and institutions as governance, democracy, universal education and health. The acceptance of education as a universal right was common to all areas which we studied, except for Burkina Faso. Whereas only a minority went to school, many of the boys and girls who did go to school did not really perceive school as a useful and necessary institution. They still had to learn to abide by the discipline imposed by the modern school and learn the alien culture which the school disseminates. Going to school means leaving behind some of the local culture and tradition and acquiring new knowledge, new values, and new codes of conduct.

Schools indeed often align neither with the life experiences nor with the expectations and needs of the children. That actually is intrinsic to the function of the educational system. Schools are carriers of modernisation and have the pedagogical function of introducing new knowledge and skills as well as new ideas and new values. If schools are not operating in the mainstream of villages which are being touched by the development process, 'modernising' influences will be limited and traditional values will prevail. Introducing appropriate education thus is not a simple problem of adjusting the educational system to the local context and the class-specific or ethnic culture. The introduction of new values through the schooling system implies that the local culture and the culture of the children entering the classroom will be altered. Modern schools introduce modernisation and rational thought.

Such introduction of new thought and knowledge should apply equally to girls and boys, to poor children and middle-class children, but this transmission will only operate if the gaps in gender and class are bridged by appropriate teaching techniques and educational content. As long as that does not happen, the relevance of education may indeed remain to be perceived as ambiguous. The study in Nicaragua observed how traditional ideas and attitudes, such as *machista,* come in conflict with modern beliefs, such as the equality of men and women and mutual respect. Secular ideas and the elimination of discrimination, as in the case of India, have a tense relationship with traditional village life, which persists with the hierarchical order of caste subordination. A complicating factor is that, more often than not, children are expected to rise above their current situations with the help of teachers who belong to a different cultural and/or ethnic group altogether. The most obvious gaps between students and teachers, concerning culture and class, were found in Burkina Faso. Pupils there are being taught French along with reading, writing, arithmetic, and science (all in French).

Poor village boys and girls enter the realm of education because they have understood the need for learning through a public institution. Once within the school, however, they have to succumb to a regime of order and discipline. Pedagogues from all backgrounds generally agree that such rigorous discipline tends to kill the imagination, sense of belonging, and self-regulation, which are three important features to develop in a child. But circumstances in classrooms are unfavourable to such lofty ideals, and usually an adult-inspired discipline is imposed from above. Such discipline is not always easy to maintain however, certainly not in classes where sixty to seventy students are cramped in a room made for thirty.

In countries like Nicaragua and Vietnam, teachers appear to be slightly closer to the population at large, as they lack the disdain and arrogance of a higher caste or class, as in India, Tanzania, or Burkina Faso. In Nicaragua or Vietnam teachers may actually go and talk to parents when problems persist, or they may use other methods, such as sending the child to the school director, grading down the marks, sending him or her home with an extra task, or, in the worst case, suspending the pupil from school. In Vietnam particularly, teachers play a vital role in improving the quality of education and are properly taught how to deal with children. Over the last few years, primary and secondary schools have received a contingent of young, healthy, and well-trained teachers to replace the old ones. Every summer vacation, these young schoolteachers have access to short-term training courses that enable them to update their knowledge and to meet the requirements of the education reforms made by the Ministry of Education and Training. When discussing the quality of teaching, parents from Quang Son commune said:

> Over the last few years, with young teachers coming from Thai Nguyen, the teaching quality here has been improved. We feel at ease when we hear the children commending their teachers. During parents' meetings,

the school also reported to us about the teaching and learning quality, which has been improved year after year.

Children will not always appreciate the discipline and the strict maintenance of school hours; it leaves them little room for choice and decision making. The learning environment refers to an attitude that emerges gradually and that in Vietnam had progressed much further than, for example, in Burkina Faso where we met many boys and girls who could not really appreciate the rigour of the school system. As a fourteen-year-old girl in Batie said:

> At school one has only to do what the teachers asks you, you cannot say no; sometimes the teacher make us do things we do not want to do at that time e.g., cleaning the school yard or the classes. You have to come on time and leave when they ask you to leave the school; in many things we do not have a choice.

Children thus may be irregular in attendance because they fancy neither the teaching nor the teachers. Unfortunately, that problem also exists with teachers. A different problem affecting the quality of education indeed is the fact that teachers often do not show up. There are various reasons for this. Teachers may be underpaid (and take on more jobs), they may have been appointed in distant rural areas (and prefer to stay in the cities), they may lack the teaching skills (and only cash the salaries), they may have to teach children who belong to a poor (and despised) caste or ethnic group (whom one does not want to mingle with), etc. For example, the study found that in Bolivia, many evening school teachers were forced to take on additional jobs. One teacher explained: 'Our salary for teaching in one school is not sufficient to support our families. Therefore we are forced to do other jobs on the side'. However, working two jobs brings with it a new set of problems. One teacher commented that 'my students have a lot of problems, because they are from very poor families. But sometimes I am so tired of the work I do during the day, that I forget, and get mad at them for not paying attention'. Additionally, working two jobs can lead to absenteeism. In Santa Cruz and in El Torno, around 30% of the children in the evening schools stated that tardiness and nonattendance are the most negative aspects of their teachers (Moreno 2002, 98 and 160). It was not entirely surprising to encounter children in the evening schools who could hardly read or write.

Although children agree with the teachers that a good education is important for their future, some children unsurprisingly express the view that 'school is boring, you have to do maths, you have to do that, you have do this'. Time passes quickly if the subject is interesting, if the children like the teacher, or if they are allowed to work together with friends. If the subject does not interest them, time passes very slowly. This was a general observation made in every region of the study. Children, for understandable reasons, as one girl in Batie stated, find the classes 'soooo boring. The teacher never asks us a single thing. She just stands there talking.' Interactive approaches in the classrooms are indeed a rare thing. The study found that the most common ways of teaching are reading loudly from the textbooks or writing the lessons on the blackboard and having the children copy them, or, in other words, a very 'top-down' method. Despite all the discussion on education and the need to reach universal enrolment, the very teaching methods hardly ever have seemed to come in for modification or public debate. In the ex-colonial countries, it tends to continue in the same manner in which teaching was done during colonial times. The lack of interaction results in boredom among the students, and this in turn leads to disruptive behaviour which again entices rigorous disciplinary methods.

A number of children reported that they were punished mentally as well as physically in the classroom. Children in Bolivia complained of being called names like 'stupid' (*zonzo*), 'donkey' (*burro*), and 'a good for nothing' (*un inútil*) 'who will never learn' (*nunca vas a apprender*). Physical punishments include beatings to the back and buttocks with a cane, belt, or whip, whilst the child stands bent over with hands on the floor (a punishment called *al chancho*, the pig's way), beatings to the hands with a cane, beatings to the face with an open hand, and so on. In Tanzania children also reported physical and psychological abuse. According to a boy in Mwanza, teachers often get angry and beat the children to silence them:

> Teachers are beating pupils. Most of the teachers are very harsh. They do not want to help children. If someone fails to answer a question in class instead of the teacher helping the pupil to correct the mistakes, he or she beats the pupil. Some of them beat students using big sticks and that causes a lot of pain. Some of the pupils do not come to school because they want to avoid punishment.

Children in urban Dar told us that kids, after they have been out of school for a long time, do not want to come back to school because they are afraid of being punished by teachers. 'It is normal for pupils who are skipping school to be beaten by teachers once they are back. To avoid this children stay at home unless they have a good reason for having been absent'. These children added that parents, if they notice that their child is not showing up at school, actually ask teachers to beat their child more often to prevent truancy. If a parent would object to the beatings it wouldn't help much, because, 'beating is a school rule' and is 'just a way of teaching'. It is a story we heard across the countries. In addition to beatings, some teachers resort to strong language when scolding the boys, or give punishments such as forcing them to stand in the corner the whole day, or give them bad marks. Most of the schoolboys are evidently full of pent-up anger because of this too-severe treatment.

Students' complaints about unjust treatment involved more than verbal and physical abuse. They also mentioned the unwillingness of the teachers to listen to their argument, or their side of the story. When the children were asked what they would like their teachers to be like, they answered that they would like teachers to be communicative (*que nos escuchen*), friendly, caring, creative, and that they would like the relationship between student and teacher to be a mature one. Jherson (twelve) in rural Bolivia, possibly voiced the opinion of many when he explained, 'as a teacher one should not beat children, one should talk with them, explain them things. And if we do not understand they should explain it again. One does not understand better by getting beaten, you know'.

Jherson's words are a truth that many teachers are not prepared to accept. They appear to justify regimental discipline and physical punishment with 'cultural' arguments, as the following testimony of an evening school teacher in El Alto shows: 'At home they are also punished like this; so, if they don't listen, you have to use the language they are used to'. In a sense, he is correct. Many parents are short of time to properly educate their children. Parents or other adults are too busy making a living; the time they spend on their children has become very limited. Some parents go without speaking to their children for a whole week, as they leave for work when their children are still asleep and only return home after the children have gone to bed. This lack of interaction results in a generation gap, where adults impose their viewpoints onto children and judge children's behaviour without proper evidence, without taking the time, or without having the time, to talk. Instead of giving advice or reasoning, they resort to scolding and beating to threaten the children and to force them to do as the parents wish. In the words of the director of the evening school *Mario Guzman Aspiazu* in Bolivia: 'When one has to work all day, like the parents of these children, it is more time effective to use physical force to explain the difference between good and bad'.

There, however, is a difference. Children usually dare not run away from the family (although studies of street children indicate that violence at home, rather than poverty, was a major reason for abandoning the family). When a child faces violence and abuse in school, the very place which should be child friendly, dropping out becomes a stark option. We have seen earlier that the mother of Jherson explained that the son often abstained from going to school because he had to work on the farm. We were not sure whether that work on the farm necessarily had to interfere with school. We now learn from Jherson himself that he did experience violence in school and that this possibly is the real reason why he abstains more often than he should. Attributing the absence from school to the violence and humiliation would mean a public confession of defeat and powerlessness; attributing it to the need to contribute to the household confers the idea of agency and as such a positive handling of the situation. Dropping out is usually due to a multiplicity of reasons. Even when parents indicate that work at home or financial constraints are the reason for not attending school, the real cause may often be found within the school itself.

Sufficient finances, good policy, and good governance are often mentioned as the essential prerequisites for achieving universal education. Who, however, is responsible for stimulating children to come to school in the first place? The role of parents, and sometimes teachers, in preventing children from dropping out was mentioned remarkably often by the children who did attend school. In Mwanza and Ifakara, we heard the following remarks, which all centred around the idea that there should be more supervision:

> Parents should follow up on their children and know exactly what they are doing in school. Parents need to know how their children are progressing and should talk with the teachers. Teachers never see the parents.

> I think teachers, children, and parents should work together. Parents should make sure that their children are going to school; at the same time teachers should inform parents immediately if their children are not coming to school.

> Parents need to be very close with their children. This is also because there are some pupils who lie to their parents that they have been to school while they have not been. Other parents know that their children are not going to school, but they don't take any measures against their children.

> People of the community should help. When any child of school age is seen in the street, adults should bring him back to school.

These were children who had been reared by their parents with good values. They appreciated the guidance given by adults and actually by doing so questioned the self-acclaimed rights of child liberation. Participation for them was entering the school system and behaving orderly, as told by the adults. They wished other children had a similar family structure with caring parents.

Children not attending school usually had a different story to tell. They explained that they had to work, that school was too expensive, or too far away, and that teachers were unbearable, driving children out of the classroom. These children mentioned not the parents, but the government, as responsible for getting children into school. Such perceptions were more prevalent in Nicaragua and Bolivia and in some areas of India, where political consciousness was more apparent. Marina, a fifteen-year-old girl attending the evening school in Cochabamba, Bolivia, stated: 'Our school is in such a bad state because the mayor does not care about the children, he only cares about robbing money, about filling his pockets'. Such accusations were often heard. Thirteen-year-old Mario, attending the evening school in El Torno, was even more resentful: 'The politicians talk and talk but they never accomplish anything. They only care about themselves, but they do not think about the marginal neighbourhoods, they never come here to see how bad our school is'. Elvira (thirteen), who attends the day school in Cochabamba, explained:

> It is our mayor, Manfred Reyes Villa, who is to blame for the bad state our school is in. He came to our school five years ago and promised to renovate our school. Our school was in a terrible state, we could not even pass classes here: the roof was broken, so we were sitting in the rain, when it rained and in the heat when there was sun. The seats and benches were broken. Nevertheless, we are still waiting for Manfred Reyes Villa to accomplish the things he promised us. He has done absolutely nothing, except for building his second big house here in Cochabamba.

These children blame the (local) government for the bad facilities. They consider it the responsibility of the government to improve the condition of the schools and to see to it that the children are able to learn. The children regret they can't make those changes themselves: 'This is a government school, so the government is responsible. We do not have the means, how could we pay for these changes?'

5.4. WHY DO CHILDREN GO TO SCHOOL?

The research question usually is why children do not go to school. The question could be framed differently: why do children go to school, which after all is an alien institution and which interferes with the daily activities of traditional childhood.

One reason why children go to school, and stay in school, is the realization that the knowledge they get is useful. There appears to be a general eagerness among the pupils to learn. Although the quality of many schools needs considerable improvement and although many teachers are not an inspiring lot, children felt that they learned new things. Reading, writing, and calculating were obviously mentioned as the effect of being in school, but school also provided other bits of knowledge. In general, if given the chance, pupils are interested in going to school and benefiting from the teachers. Not all teachers are equally inspiring and the children are taking it in their strides. In Vietnam for example, the overall impression was that pupils were reasonably satisfied with the commitment of their teachers. A group of schoolgirls from Phuc Xa lower secondary school stated their opinion as follows: 'Some teachers are interesting, some are dull, but most of them are interesting teachers.'

Table 5.1 Children's Assessment of Education in Vietnam (%)

	9–12 age group	*13–16 age group*
Very helpful	80.0	72.2
A little helpful	18.3	23.7
Obtain nothing after learning	0.8	1.5
Don't know	0.8	2.5

In our survey, on an average, 75% of the child interviewees said 'knowledge obtained from school is very helpful in life', 22% said that it is 'a little helpful', and only 1% said that they 'obtain nothing after learning'. So we can see that, when good education is provided, most children think knowledge provided by school to be helpful. This shows a certain success of school education. Especially the younger children think highly of school education. The learning environment and the attitude of the teachers help to generate a love for learning and help to develop their personality.

Education is basically seen by children as a way to improve their living conditions, to 'get a better future'. The education might prepare them for no more than a menial job in the city; but even such a job will enable them to send funds home. But parents also seem to realise that education helps the children to speak properly (and even other languages, such as French in Burkina Faso), to read and write, to make calculations, and to acquire good manners and life knowledge. Those involved in the study in all regions stressed the significance of education, and gave the following reasons, which are encompassing and go beyond the functional role which the educational system appears to have acquired in the present-day market-oriented thinking:

- It allows them to learn basic abilities such as reading, writing, and mathematical operations.
- It permits them to establish new social relations with classmates and teachers.
- It helps them to acquire qualities and moral values such as solidarity and responsibility.
- It provides greater opportunities to improve their economic situation and support their families by getting remunerative work.

Whereas finances or the need of the child to contribute to the work in the household may play a crucial role, it is usually the attitude of the parents that becomes the deciding factor. The children usually have high aspirations, whether overtly or secretly. One of the questions we asked the children was related to their hopes and dreams for the future. In Nicaragua, for example, although ultimately only 12% of young men and women have access to higher education, the majority of children and adolescents wish to become graduated professionals. In Tanzania, practically each and every child immediately answered: 'secondary school!' Only by finishing primary school and going to secondary school did they see a way to a brighter future. With secondary education they could get an official job and earn some money. They said that if they could not get into a secondary school, they would probably stay at home to help their parents. If given the option though, most children would prefer to continue studying. From the survey in Bolivia we learned that more than 80% of the children aspired to continue studying (Moreno 2002, 169 and 108).

The relationship between education and a 'better future' sometimes referred to the contribution which good education could make to social development. Some children thought that their future would enable them to do good for society or to change the present political and economical situation in their country. Fourteen-year-old Martin in Bolivia expressed this 'postponed agency': 'We as children, are the future of Bolivia. We have to go to the university, so that we can tell that the politicians are doing badly, that they have to make things right'. In addition, we found many children who wanted to become doctors, lawyers, nurses, teachers, or police constables. The explanation for aspiring for such a future (which was unrealistic anyway) was not so much the idea of having a good job with good money but rather the social service. By becoming a lawyer, one could defend the poor people in court, by becoming a doctor one could bring health services to the villages, and by becoming a constable, one could act against the rich miscreants and corrupt politicians, etc.

Nevertheless, the majority of the children regard education as a tool for upward mobility, so that 'we will not become like our parents'. Juana, eleven, also from Cochabamba, stated: 'My father never had an education. Now he is a taxi driver. And I see how he is suffering, that he has to make great efforts to earn 1 boliviano. I do not want to end up like that. I want to be able to support my family, therefore I am studying'. The following words of Javier (fifteen, El Alto, Bolivia) further confirm this sentiment:

> I am determined to study until I am an architect or a lawyer or a doctor. I do not want to end up like my father. He suffers badly. He works a lot for little money and he does not have stable work, sometimes he works, sometimes not. And plasterers also have accidents, some die while at work. Therefore I want to study, to not to be in the same situation as my father.

In general, children attending evening school, i.e., those working during the day, gave more substantial reasons for studying, in comparison with others. They were noticeably more determined about their choices. By attending evening school, working children hope to achieve increased access to the labour market and secure a more desirable social and economic position. Marina, for example, stated that a boss would certainly yell at her if she were without a degree, but 'when I have a degree he will not do that anymore, he will respect me because I will have a degree'.

The point about improving one's economic position, and helping one's family, is also a consideration for the younger children who are already conscientious of the economic difficulties within their household, which they would like to help ease. The following statements, recorded in Nicaragua, illustrate this importance ascribed to education:

> I like to learn so many different things. It is going to help me to get a job and to help my mama (A.Z., nine years)

> Here we learn to read, to write, to keep friends and possibly later to be in a learned profession (I.V., eleven years)

> It is important because by learning I may become somebody later in life and help my parents (D.L., thirteen years)

> To me it means improvement and a better future because I want to become someone in life and to do the work I like (M.A., fifteen years)

The belief in going to school to get a good job in the future is also held in the countryside. Most children in poor rural families work in agriculture, and receiving a good education is often seen as an escape from this life. The study in the countryside found that education and migration are often related: 61% of the children included in the El Torno study intend to migrate and education is treated as a means to this end. Not only the children, but also the parents, used the desire to migrate 'to a better future' as a validation of studying. The following statement of a father in El Alto, Bolivia, illustrates this:

> I want Edgar to have a good education, so that he will not become like me. With a good education he will be able to have a stable job and to maintain his future family. It will prevent him from the sufferings that I had to go through. Only children that study have the opportunity to earn a decent living and therefore a better future than they would have here in the countryside.

Education has yet another appeal. Making friends is an important bonus for children who go to school. Twelve-year-old Halimatou from Batie said that, since there are no playing facilities in the school, 'the only thing we can do is to sit under the trees and chat and chat, but it is nice to be with friends'. And Harouna, a thirteen-year-old boy from Dem, added: 'At school there is a lot of work to do all the day but still we can play and enjoy ourselves. I think the school is better than home in that, at home you cannot play much and there are no friends around.'

In rural areas, such as in Dem and Batie, the school day is sometimes the only opportunity to meet people from other villages. The majority of girls interviewed stressed the importance of lunchtime as a time for being with their friends. Zienabou, a fifteen-year-old girl from Batie, said: 'My parents do not allow me to visit my friends in the other villages; besides I have a lot of things to do when I come back from school. Going to school means that I am free to play with my friends. They have so many new things to tell me. I learn a lot.' Thanks to the school, children have social relations not only with their family members, but also with their school friends and their teachers. But the time that they are able to spend with other children is usually very limited. The children are either at home, where they normally do not have time to play or visit with other children, or they are at school, under the teacher's supervision. The limited time and space available to them to socialise with other children is just one reason why classes are sometimes often chaotic: children talking to each other, running in and out the classroom, playing football in the hall, and so on. This, as mentioned earlier, was especially the case in the evening schools in Bolivia. David (fourteen), who works in a sewing atelier in El Alto, said, 'after a day's work, who wants to listen to the teacher. I prefer to catch up with my friends, whom I haven't seen all day'. For him, meeting friends was probably the most important function of school, but school authorities do not realize that they have such a function. Children attend class with concerns other than education. Many working children show up for class exhausted and with an empty stomach; furthermore, all they desire is to see their friends. Teachers are, however, focussed on supplying education, not solutions to other problems the children may be experiencing. The educators ignore the additional requirements of the children, and thus, the function of the school is defined unilaterally. In this light, the chaos created by the children is a form of agency, an expression that they do not share the teacher's vision of their needs. By creating chaos, the children attempt to express that their needs to 'be with friends' and to consume the food provided are more important than the education. Linking the chaos inside the classrooms to the specific needs of the working children, can also explain why the chaos was worse in the evening schools.

5.5. EDUCATION AND GENDER

Most adults whom we interviewed thought it was equally important for boys and girls to get educated. Many respondents had trouble though explaining why it was important; they eventually resorted to 'it is the child's right' and therefore their parental duty to send both sons and daughters to school. Other people were able to articulate the view that an educated girl would receive more respect and could contribute more to her family, that girls are as competent as boys for jobs, and that girls should be able to depend on themselves in case the husband dies or divorces her. Some respondents mentioned education being even more important for girls than for boys because it is harder for girls to get jobs without an education and because girls are more likely to help their parents in the future.

The politically correct assertion that both boys and girls should have equal access to school is not always reflected in actual behaviour. Most of the school dropouts are girls, including some girls who were performing well at school. Moreno notes in the Bolivian case that the gender division of 'helping' causes the parents of the girls to take them out of school at an early stage: 'according to collected testimonies, the marginal position of girls in the school is directly related to their active and important participation in and around the household. In general the girls leave their study because they have to help in the household and/or do other jobs outside the house' (Moreno 2002, 93). In most areas, the tradition was that girls from a young age onwards had to be socialized into doing household work. Daughters, particularly the eldest daughters, had an essential function in running the household and looking after the younger children. As a saying in Vietnam goes, 'fertile field and she-buffalo are not worth the eldest daughter'.

Often a different plan has been made for the daughters, namely to get married, have babies, raise them, and serve her husband and his family. This may not be the role perception of the majority of parents anymore, but tradition does persist. Dropping out or truancy may also be caused by the inability of these parents to pay the tuition fee for all of their children, when the traditional attitude towards girls make the parents decide in favour of education for the boy. That attitude these days applies less to the primary school—most parents realize that daughters also have the right to basic education—but much more to the secondary school. Especially parents who have had only a minimal level of education consider it sufficient when girls complete the primary school or the junior secondary school. This was apparent in Bolivia, where Llamos (2001, 57) observed:

> The heads of the families are convinced that the girls only have to go to school to a certain level. The majority of the parents think that since the girls finally are going to end up serving their husbands, it is enough when they go to school to learn how to live in the city, to attend the household and their business.

According to the tradition in many countries, also in Vietnam, parents are responsible for arranging their children's marriages. Parents worry about getting the wedding of their daughters arranged before they get 'too old' or before '*trot dai*' (pregnancy before marriage). This sentiment is still common in the rural and mountainous areas, and helps to explain why getting married is a priority for girls, whereas boys are motivated to keep studying for as long as they can manage. Presently, however, most families seem to have come around to the idea of encouraging intelligent children in their studies, irrespective of gender. Two remarks made by girls in La Son:

> Now it is different, study is so hard and difficult, but both boys and girls who can study well will keep studying; the others are bad in studying must stay at home.

> In my family, it is the same. Girls can study better than boys can, and my father said: 'We must try to find money to support all of you in your studies. Who does not want to study can stay at home and if their life is not good, they must not complain about their parents later'.

Within the schools, gender does not appear to be an obvious discriminating factor. Girls mainly do better than boys, who are often subject to teachers' scolding, beating, and discipline. Studies show that schoolgirls practically everywhere are hard learning, hard working, more docile, and more disciplined. Boys may sometimes have better school results because girls have to do more housework than boys. However, having to spend more time on household work does not necessarily interfere with the studies. The Headmaster of Quang Son lower secondary school, Mr. Dam Van C., said that girls work very hard and have no time to learn, they in fact have more potential than boys and are not so distracted by playing as boys are:

> In my school, girls' learning performance is better than boys. The girls learn very quickly in class, but they are allowed less time to spend on studying. At home they have to work harder than boys who are more engrossed in playing. The buffalo girls take textbooks with them to learn, while the buffalo boys don't. However, parents often ask their daughters to drop out when they go to upper secondary school because the school is far from home.

Interviews with schoolchildren also show a better relationship between teachers and schoolgirls than with boys. We were often told by the girls, like this group of twelve- to thirteen-year-old girls in Phuc Xa commune, that 'in class, girls are doing better, because they learn harder and concentrate more on the lecture. The boys are lazier and play football very often. Although some boys are learning well, many others are lazy.' They themselves were sometimes scolded, but they were never beaten: 'Our teachers only scold or remind us. Sometimes they call us to a private corner to remind us of our mistakes when we forget to bring our books and notebooks from home, or when we are gossiping'. Schoolgirls in La Son commune also affirmed not being beaten by their teachers. They were just reminded, criticised, had their names noted in the teacher's book or requested to write a self-criticism. However, a group of schoolboys, aged thirteen to sixteen in La Son, told us that the teacher had beaten them all at least once: 'We played football and came in class late. My teacher called each of us in and slapped us in our faces. Our teacher even forced me to kneel on the rock, until the skin on my knee was grazed.'

Even in Vietnam, where gender discrimination was less, a number of parents clearly had different perspectives on the future of their children. Our findings show that boys and girls from the three project sites all have a similar learning capacity, but that since girls were more serious in their studies, they made up a large percentage of the excellent students. Unfortunately though, some girls cannot always continue higher education; whereas 5.4% of the households explicitly stated to intend to let their sons enjoy higher education, not a single household showed such intent for their daughters.

An eleven-year-old girl in La Son stopped going to school after grade five, and we asked her why she dropped out: 'I have to take care of my younger siblings and harvest rice.' Her younger sister, Hien, dropped out while she was in grade three in order to help transport rice. Her younger brothers did not need to drop out: 'They have to go to school. Boys must have a career.' Despite a girl's sadness and objections, parents don't change their minds. Some girls even think it is their responsibility to drop out and give their brothers the chance to continue in their place. If they start working, then their brothers can go to school. A sixteen-year-old girl in Quang Son explained:

> There are five people in my family, my grandmother, my mother, my two younger brothers and I. My father died in 1990. I'm the elder daughter. I had to drop out from school to work and help my mother support my two brothers' schooling. I work at the quarry and earn 22.000 dong per day. I give my mother 12.000 dong and keep 10.000 dong. When there is no work at the quarry, I work for hire in picking tea leaves and earn 10.000 dong per day. I don't want to leave school, but my brothers shouldn't be forced to drop out because they are boys.

CONCLUSION

The accounts of children and their parents have carried the message that the value of education in most areas is not in doubt. In general, possibly with the exception of one area which we studied in an isolated village close to the Sahel in Burkina Faso, the equation of childhood with education is by and large accepted. The nonachievement of the millennium development goals by 2015, not even the limited objective of achieving universal primary education, is not because of the failure to convince the parents or the children to go to school. Practically all children and parents told us that education helps children to prepare for a better future, it develops their talents, increases job opportunities, and it gives children time for socialising and playing with other children. However, at the same time, we noted that not all children are in school. Especially the villages in Burkina Faso, Tanzania, and India actually still have a bleak record. This chapter has shown the different reasons that explain this contradiction between a general wish for education and the actual levels of attendance.

The first cluster of reasons comprises factors *within* the school territory. We have seen that poor conditions of school facilities are acutely experienced as a hindrance to proper studies. When children have to sit in cramped rooms, without much ventilation in the stagnant summer heat and with broken-glass windows in the biting winter cold, or with only a worn-out blackboard as an educational support tool, children and parents sometimes prefer their children to stay at home. On the other hand, children mentioned how adequate school facilities are factors that create an inviting learning environment. Proximity and accessibility of schools is also important in getting children into schools, and keeping them there. Since some school buildings would be appropriate only to function as a cattle shed, one could not really expect children to be attracted to come and enjoy sitting there on the bare and dusty floor.

Another factor affecting school attendance is the quality of education. We observed that children negatively experience top-down methods of teaching. The usual way of teaching in all the schools involves the teacher writing the lessons on the blackboard and the children copying these lessons. The absence of interaction in the classrooms results in boredom among the students, which in turn may result in unruliness and truancy. Additionally, the children reported that the education which they receive does not conform to their perceived needs. For example, respectively 39% of the boys and 61% of the girls in the survey population in Vietnam complained about the lack of vocational training which they consider important, especially for those who are not able to continue their education at upper secondary school level. The schools still follow a traditional teaching method, which focuses on theory while neglecting vocational training. In addition, the children are frequently taught by teachers who belong to different cultural and/or ethnic groups, which can also result in a feeling of nonbelonging which ultimately can lead to dropping out, especially if it combines with derogatory remarks. Lastly, the rampant verbal and physical abuse encountered in school classrooms indeed is a major reason for children to stay way.

The second cluster of reasons that affect children in their school life stems from their lives *outside* the school realm. The socioeconomic situation of a family is most vital to the continuation of a child's education. First of all, poverty makes it very difficult to afford everything the child needs to go to school. Many parents informed us they were unable to pay school enrolment fees, examination fees, pens, books, the costs for cleaning the school, the costs for attending parent meetings, school uniforms, travelling to and from school, and so forth. Poverty can also result in poor performances by the children, as they come to class hungry. Poverty as such will usually not act as the only prohibiting factor. While some children did go to school, and did not use poverty as an argument, other children of equally poor families never attended or dropped out, using poverty as an argument. In such cases, it is not uncommon to blame the egoism and shortsightedness of the parents. From the point of view of the child and the parents, however, it could also rather be a rational choice. Poverty will be one of the variables shaping that choice. Other aspects may reinforce such a choice and in the end may keep the child out of school. These aspects relate to the functioning of the school and include bad teaching and physical and mental punishment. The bad features in a school system will have worse effects on the poorest children who outside the classroom and inside the classroom are the most marginalised and most despicable among all the children. The choice not to go to school among the poor often reflects such a feeling of discrimination and nonbelonging.

Poverty can also lead to child labour, which also has a direct effect on education. Many children stated they did not attend school or missed classes because they had to supplement the family income or help the family in household tasks. The phenomena of child labour also influences the school life of children in other ways; children come to school tired, as they have been working all day, and many children come to school to meet with friends, as they lack affection on the work floor. In other words, the socioeconomic situation of the parents can result in a child having more urgent requirements than education. The children show up at school with a need for food, sleep, attention, and affection. Education comes at a distant last place. These basic needs, resulting from conditions outside the school realm, produce chaos in the classroom, absenteeism and school dropouts, particularly if the teachers are usually unaware of the many jobs which children have at home and which in fact means that children cannot live up to the role model of a childhood only devoted to study and play. Since teachers by and large come from middle-class families, the multiple roles which children bring into the classroom are usually not understood and always never given attention to.

Although parents claim to find education equally important for girls and for boys, most school dropouts are girls; even girls who performed well at school. This gender difference can be explained by economic as well as cultural arguments. First of all, most parents are more concerned with their daughter's ability to help out in the house and in the field. This is especially true for the most deprived families, which also happen to be the households where the parents have low, or no, levels of education. Whereas daughters often had to stop going to school when their services were needed at home, sons only had to stop studying when the parents were in absolute poverty. Secondly, traditional gender roles prevent girls from successfully completing their studies in higher grades. It is in most cases still considered more important for a girl to prepare for a future in which she serves her husband and looks after the children, rather than for one in which she has her own career. The normative prescription that boys and girls should be treated equally has percolated down into the villages, and a minimum level of education is made available to the girls as well, but since girls usually would not go in for a career later in life, it does not seem appropriate to most parents to invest in secondary education. The norm—gender equality in education—is at loggerheads with the limited economic dynamism in many rural societies and with the continuing traditional roles which men and women have. The vision of a different role model is only slowly penetrating village life and its further spread is hampered by the existing role models. It is a rational choice, if a choice is to be made, to send the boy rather than the girl. The limited economic dynamism allows the gender discrimination to linger on.

This chapter also gave an idea of how parents and children see solutions to the problems encountered in the school realm. The government is often quoted as the responsible party in getting children into school and some children consciously blame the government for the bad condition the public schools are in and for the poor quality of education provided in these schools. The study found that an appropriate government and/or NGO policy helps children to come to school. It appears that if the children are targeted by interventions by the government, and in some cases aided by voluntary agencies, the gender gap can be overcome. It also appears that improvements in the availability of schools in the neighbourhood result in higher school enrolment. The case study of Rajasthan, at the beginning of this chapter, reveals that when advocacy for education is brought to poorer neighbourhoods, the impact is remarkable. The night school started by an NGO has given crucial opportunities to girls, so that they are now able to attend school after completing their daily household chores. Nevertheless, public schools in poor areas are often short of funds, affecting the education of children. The parents also commented on the bad state of public schools and often expressed their desire to send their children to a private school, where the education is considered to be better. But finances prevent them from doing so, thereby completing the circle of poverty: economically deprived families are forced to send their children to poorly run public schools where the education is of a low standard and therefore future perspectives for a better life are limited. Opting out may then appear as a rational choice. The push-out (of the child by the school system) may often appear as a pull-out (by the child and its parents from school).

6   Child Labour

The issue of child labour has become a controversial issue, not only among researchers and social activists, but also among the parents and the children themselves (Boyden, Ling and Myers 1998, Lieten and White 2001, Lieten 2002a). In the course of their upbringing many children work, and such work may be considered a healthy process of socialisation. But, especially in developing countries, quite a number of children are heavily exploited through their work and are unable to attend school. These conditions have led to a forceful demand for a total elimination of child labour. Total elimination is indeed an appropriate policy for exploitative and impairing forms of child labour, but we should not forget to differentiate between exploitative forms of child labour and work that does not hamper a child's social, physical, and mental development.

The previous two chapters have shed light on the daily activities of some of the children living in slums and villages. We have seen that children are indeed quite active throughout the day, engaging in activities that could be classified as work but that need not necessarily be impairing forms of child labour. The work that children often do, such as looking after their younger siblings, doing household work, assisting their parents in the field, tending buffaloes, or cutting grass, is mostly helpful for the development of the child. It is not uncommon to highlight the positive aspects of such work and stress that it is part of local tradition. A study (Save the Children 1997, 7–8) commented on the wide diversity of work done by children and the important role of their work for the household:

> Children's work is an essential resource in the livelihood strategies of poor rural households who often would not be able to make ends meet without children's help. Children's work reproduces rural society with its divisions of labour and allocation of responsibilities. It partially develops children's personalities and defines their roles in society. Through working, children acquire the skills and knowledge they will need as adults.

Children indeed acquire skills and insights through work activities, but the system also reproduces the labour division in society. Children will continue the type of work that their own fathers and mothers were doing, particularly if that work preempts proper schooling and leisure. Behind the work that children are doing, within the context of family life, always lurks the danger of child labour. 'Child labour' as a concept refers only to those children who have to work as if they were adults and who are engaged in such work for such a long time and under such conditions that their normal development as a child is impaired and that it interferes with education. In cases of child labour, children have to do such work, which is detrimental to their mental and physical health, in order to supplement the family income or to replace one of the adult family members in the household (Lieten 2002b and 2005). The central issue in the case of working children is education. As long as the (limited) contributions of children to the household or to economic activities do not interfere with the comprehensive development of their personality, work need not be objectionable. In this chapter we shall try to get a better understanding of the work and labour that children do.

6.1. HELPING IN THE HOUSEHOLD

Children working in and around the household are the rule rather than the exception in the countries which we studied. This work is partly a consequence of 'need' and a direct response by the children in their awareness of family poverty or hardship. The fact that children work can in itself be seen as a form of agency. By working, they help to alleviate the poverty of their families. Doing so allows them to break away from some social constraints. For example, children whose families do not have enough money to pay for their school fees can work to pay their own way, thus enabling some of them access to education that would have otherwise been out of reach.

The children were willing to take on a greater responsibility in the household but this willingness was not always without ambivalence. Sometimes, it is a combination of coercion and free choice. The case of Hussein, a thirteen-year-old boy from Tanzania, does well as an example. We met him in front of his house, along a steep and twisting, dirty rocky road in urban Mwanza, where he was selling coffee to passersby. Hussein has two younger sisters. Their father died and when their mother could not take care of them anymore, she sent them to live with their grandfather. Hussein told us that he sells coffee for his grandfather, while his sisters clean the house, wash the dishes, and prepare dinner. He does this every day after school for three hours. If he refuses, his grandfather yells at him. He doesn't get paid; the money he earns he hands over to his grandfather. But he says he doesn't mind. He likes helping the family and because of his help, he and his sisters can go to school.

Despite the occasional frustration, the children seemed to autonomously take on considerable responsibilities, reasserting solidarity with the family members. For example, Sasosna, a fifteen-year-old boy from Batie (Burkina Faso), said: 'I work to support my whole family; my parents are old and I'm the eldest, so I work and live with my brothers and sisters here until they can support themselves.' Another thirteen-year-old boy in the same area said:

> I was compelled to leave school last year because my father was sick. I have many brothers and sisters and so I have to take care of the animals and the garden with my other brothers. If we want to survive, we have to support each other. My father is always telling us that we should work together to help our family.

The contribution of children to the household economy is often critical for rural families. In general, the work which they do is supporting work rather than remunerative work. This applies particularly to girls (and women) whose contributions to housework and farming tend to remain outside the cash economy, even though they may work harder and longer hours than their male cohorts.

In contrast to the concept of labour, the children use the concept of 'helping' when defining the tasks they perform within the family domain. 'Helping' can take on two forms. It can mean: helping a family member outside the house in his or her work; for example sowing and harvesting together with the family on the family land or a child mixing the cement for his father who is a plasterer. It can also mean helping family members inside the house in the household tasks. The fact that 'helping', as opposed to going out to work, does take place within the family context, may be one of the reasons why 'helping' is considered more positive than working. However, much 'helping' in many cases could be clarified as child labour.

'Helping' long hours and doing heavy work within the direct family context is often born out of economic compulsions, as shown in the following examples. The parents of Juan (fifteen) are almost never at home. Juan explained: 'My mother and father have to work constantly to get some money to eat. In the meanwhile, who will look after my younger brothers and sister? Me. So that's why I come to school in the evening.' Cesar (fourteen) attends the evening school in El Torno. During the day he helps his father who is a plasterer: 'My father is a plasterer and I help him mix the cement. Other plasterers have helpers, and they have to pay them. But because I am his son, he does not have to pay me. So that's cheap and we have more money to buy food and things like that.' Not only the children, but also the parents explained the necessity of working long hours and under hard conditions by referring to their economic conditions:

> Because there is no other work which is better paid, we all have to work. I work as a plasterer, my wife sells food to my colleagues at the work site and my children help me in my work. In this way I do not have to contract helpers. However our money is not sufficient anyway.

In the countryside of Bolivia, the necessity of children 'helping' was explained similarly. One farmer commented:

> The situation is very difficult today, there is no work and we do not earn as much as we used to. With what I earn I cannot provide for my family. This is why my wife and children have to help me. My wife sells fruit, corn, and drinks at the market. My children help her: they bring the stuff to the market and they also sell. If we were not work together, the money would not be sufficient to provide in our needs.

By and large, the children are positive about activities defined as 'helping'. They responded positively when asked if they expected their own children to help in the future. The positive connotation of 'helping' stems from the fact that, apart from remaining within the family domain, with its support and affection, children see it as a way of learning skills that can be useful later on life. Eduardo (twelve) expressed this succinctly: 'My children do not have to work. They can help their mother in the house, or help her selling in the market or at a store for example. In this way they will learn things which will serve them in future.'

A form of 'helping', which is experienced by some children as exploitative, is helping family members who are not direct members of the household. Poor families are inclined to send their children to help relatives because of the economic advantages it brings; getting a child to live with a relative, or friend of the family, is another mouth less to feed. Where the children in the countryside 'help' in accordance with their age and abilities, the children who are sent to the city to go and live with relatives have to work long hours and perform difficult tasks considering their age. In the words of schoolmaster Mario Guzman Aspiazu in El Alto, 'this custom has become the function of lending out a cheap labour force'.

A striking example is that of Julio in El Alto. His parents left him to work with his uncle and aunt in La Paz. In addition to his schoolwork (evening school), he has to help his uncle in his garage. He 'helps' there ten hours a day, performing heavy tasks, like scrubbing the paint of the cars. The children of his uncle are of the same age, but do not have to help that much and are able to attend day school. Julio defines his situation as 'highly unfair'. Another reason why he negatively experiences the work at his uncle's place is that it takes him away from his immediate family, leaving him bereft of his parents' and siblings' love and affection. The system makes the children more vulnerable to abuse and exploitation. In the words of Victor (twelve) who works ten hours a day in a garage in La Paz:

> My work sometimes makes me cry. All the time you are working, they will not let you go out to see your family or friends for one single moment. I am just sitting there all the time by myself. Therefore I am

happy when I can leave for my house and visit my brothers and can see my mum.

Children in the household have a critical support role in relieving adults from time-consuming and lowly remunerated work, such as household work, child minding, or taking care of animals. The support they give allows adults to concentrate their efforts on higher income work, for example wage work. Wage labour is becoming increasingly widespread in rural areas, not only among adults, but also among children. Generally, however, participation in wage work by children appears to be related to defective family structures, e.g., the absence of a father or a mother who could otherwise have earned the money needed for expenses such as school fees. One young girl (eleven), living in rural Mwanza (Tanzania) where she helps her mother with household jobs during the day, gave the following reason for not being able to go to school:

My dad died when I was still very young. Now my mother has to take care of me and my brothers and sisters all by herself. She does not earn enough money to pay for the school expenses; that is why I can't go to school and so I help my mother in the household.

Children in such families themselves were often aware of the fact they had to work to survive: 'hardly any income', 'hardly any sales', 'no work' and 'low wages' were references which we often heard. Exemplary were the words of Ricardo (fifteen) in the rural village of El Torno (Bolivia). At the age of seven, his father went away in search of work and never came back:

As I am the oldest of four brothers, I had to quit school and go to work, to take over my father's work so to say. When my father left we needed the money to eat and to send my brothers to school. So I had no choice. If one is born in a family that does not have any money, one has to work. Some have the luck that their father or mother or grandmother leaves them a great inheritance. But normally, if one gets born poor, all the family members have to work to survive.

When one of the parents dies or becomes seriously ill, the only option left for the eldest child is often to substitute for the parent. Even sick children have been reported to work for money as their family is too poor. Such is the case of Tran Van T., fifteen, from La Son commune. T., who suffers from a kidney condition, said:

My father died from kidney problems some years ago. My mother has suffered from a tumour in her belly for ten years, but we cannot afford her treatment. My six-year-old younger brother suffers from rheumatism and me, from kidney problems. I had to leave school to help my mother working in the field and selling bread. I only wish to be healthy enough to go to Hanoi to earn a living and to help my mother.

Children have different ways in which to contribute to the household economy. Although cash contributions to the family income were not generally reported, except for the impoverished families, in all regions children through their work added to the household income, although percentages differed. For example in El Torno, Bolivia, 86% of the children stated that they economically contributed to the family income; in Santa Cruz this percentage was as high as 93% (Moreno 2002, 86 and 150). In Nicaragua, 28% of the children were reported to be generating income. In Ifakara, Tanzania, many children were found to be involved with money-generating activities, like carrying bricks, working on other people's farms, and selling eggs, groundnuts, coconuts, or other foodstuffs on the streets. It mostly involved trade which they did for their parents, e.g., selling food the mother had cooked, but sometimes they worked 'for themselves', which meant that they could keep the earnings for themselves. The children use the money they earn to buy food, clothes, and school materials like pens and books. One twelve-year-old boy stated: 'If our parents don't have money, what else can we do?' Another twelve-year-old boy from a farming family stated: 'Sometimes we don't have enough money in the family. So I think it's important to help my parents, so that they can earn some more money'.

Even in Vietnam, where the government, despite the liberalisation, has kept in place substantial aspects of its social protection system and where economic progress has been substantial, the cash contribution of children was considerable. Of all the children we interviewed in Vietnam, only around one-third of the children claimed that they don't generate any income for their families. On the other hand, as many as 52% of the children said that they contributed between 10–20% of the total income of their households, and 8% said that they contributed between 30–40%. We also interviewed the parents about their children's contributions to the household income, and as many as 30% recognised the important role of children, but their estimation of the contribution was lower. Most of them said that their children contribute between 10–20% to the household income. The household tasks that the children perform vary, but the following tasks were undertaken in all countries of the study:

- cleaning, sweeping, washing, ironing, getting water
- purchasing and preparing food
- looking after other family members (toddlers and elderly)
- attending to the kitchen garden and the family shop

Of the children in Vietnam, 24% stated that their work consists of looking after babies or younger brothers or sisters, and almost 90% claimed that they also contribute to cooking and cleaning the house. A small proportion (around 6%) of the older children (13+) are involved in rather heavy work such as husking, pounding rice, and fetching water. Work by children in Vietnam seems to be in accordance with their age and health, and most parents also stated that they try to arrange sufficient time for their children to study. Mrs. Au Thi T., for example, a forty-four-year-old farmer from the Nung ethnic group in Quang Son commune who is a widow with two daughters who are doing well at school. After school, the children only do light housework such as preparing the meals, washing dishes, sweeping the house, and feeding the pigs and buffalos. They take the textbooks with them to learn while tending the buffalos (from 2–5 p.m.). At home they study from 7–9 p.m., and then go to bed. Asked about this issue, the group of parents in Lane 71, Tan Ap Street, Phuc Xa commune, said: 'At this age, their main task is learning. Learning takes all their time. They are small, and at school age, they must go to school'. They knew of some children who are sent out to work, but they generally disapproved of it:

> Although we are poor we still manage to raise them. They are going to school, so we have to take care of their needs to let them be equal to their classmates. But they just do some light work. They are not very busy working. If there are lots of thing to do, we, parents have to do ourselves.

Rural children, particularly farmers' children, are more involved in work on a daily basis since there is so much work on the farm that has to be done and for which it would be too expensive or too cumbersome to hire labour. A group of parents in Thuong Thu village, La Son commune, said:

> After school they have to prepare the meal if their parents come home late. In the afternoon, they have to do some work in the rice fields, to feed the pigs and chicken and to generally do some odd jobs here and there. They study while tending buffalos or taking care of younger sisters or brothers. The main time for study is in the evening, after dinner.

But the same group of parents in this rural neighbourhood also insisted that the life of children should be made as comfortable as possible so that they are provided 'with the best conditions to study, to make their life easier' and so that they have enough time to play. That is a general understanding, but socioeconomic conditions interfere with such resolve. An example from the same area, which illustrates how children sometimes have to work exceedingly long hours, is the case of the schoolboy Bui Gia D. (thirteen), the youngest child we found working in the stone quarry. The family only has a small plot of hilly land where they plant tea, and the family works at the quarry for eight hours a day. After school time, D. and his older brother (sixteen) assist their parents in quarrying and loading stones onto a truck.

It is hard work but they have to do it because it is the main job of their family. D. goes to school for half a day. He works at the quarry for the rest of the day and earns half of what the parents earn. In addition, D. has to weed in his family garden, prepare the meals, sweep the house, wash dishes, fetch water, and feed three pigs and twenty chickens. As D. is very busy working to earn a living, his school performance is suffering.

Most children in the survey areas were working and they did so for various reasons and the work need not have intervened with a healthy childhood development. The children did it gladly and developed a sense of responsibility and self-esteem. Some of the work, however, was hard (farm work, carrying bricks, selling food in the streets until late at night). Although even these children rarely complained about having to do these jobs when they were specifically asked about it and in fact mostly seemed proud to be contributing to the family income, their work should be classified as child labour. The compulsion to work as such need not be the criteria for deciding whether the work is child labour. Working children can be classified as child labourers if the work they do is inappropriate to their age, preempts their schooling, and impairs their physical and social development.

6.2. THE COMPULSION TO WORK:
EXAMPLES FROM INDIA

In India, it was observed in many areas that most of the child labourers started working after the death of one of the parents. They had to drop out of school in order to take up a job and contribute to the family income (Lieten et al. 2005). We encountered a harsh example of child labour in the wake of a family disaster in an urban slum in the Indian state Andhra Pradesh. Shobha had been in school for a couple of years when she had to drop out after her parents committed suicide. The girl, who had witnessed the incident, now works as a domestic help in two houses. After her morning shift, she helps her younger sisters with their studies. She bathes them, combs their hair and dresses them. She helps her grandmother with the cooking and the household shopping. In many respects, Shobha, although only twelve, is living the life of an adult, and a very responsible and efficient one at that.

Shobha arrives at the home of one of her employers, who is a teacher. At 7:15 a.m. she begins her work by sweeping and mopping the floor. She then washes the dishes after which she sips some tea. The teacher is sympathetic towards Shobha and gives her some reading lessons. At 9:00 a.m. she finishes her work and then proceeds to another house where she repeats the same chores but also washes clothes. After the work is completed, she is given a meal of *chapattis* and curry. At 11:00 a.m. she returns to her home where she also does some cleaning work. Her sisters and grandmother partake of the food received from their employers. After food her grandmother cleans up. Shobha rests for half an hour and then helps her sister with writing the letters of the English alphabet. Afterwards she practices writing numbers. Her grandmother leaves for the market to shop for some provisions. At 2:30, Shobha relaxes in front of the television and watches a soap program. When the sisters wake up, they all sit for lunch, which has been sent over to them by the relatives of the grandmother. At 3:30 p.m., she combs her hair, bathes her sisters, dresses them up, and pats their faces with powder. At 4:00 p.m., she is ready for her evening shift. First, she attends to the work at the teacher's home. She washes clothes, which takes approximately half an hour. Before leaving for the next home, she is given some snacks, which she eats. On reaching her other employer's home at 4:45 p.m., she begins by washing dishes, which takes up about fifteen minutes. She is back home at 5:30 p.m. She has a bath after which she plays with her sisters. At 5:45 p.m., she starts preparing dinner. She cooks rice and curry; the vegetables are chopped by her grandmother. By 6:30 p.m., Shobha finishes all her work and relaxes by chatting with her friends in the neighbourhood. The family eats at 7:30 p.m. and goes to bed at 8:00 p.m.

In New Delhi, we came across a comparable case. Iqbal (thirteen) lives with his mother and elder brother in the Govindpuri slum area. Since his mother is too sick to attend to the household chores, Iqbal has to look after himself, wash his clothes, prepare the morning cup of tea, wash the dishes, and shop for the household provisions. Iqbal is fond of video games and is a frequent visitor at his friend Vijay's home who owns a video console. However, nowadays, since the death of his father, he does not get much free time. In addition to tending to his ailing mother, Iqbal works as a helper in a motor mechanic shop. He leaves for work at around 9:30 a.m. and returns home about ten hours later. Iqbal's elder brother is a cycle mechanic. Together, they earn a paltry sum of Rs. 2,800 per month, which amounts to Rs. 31 per day per family member, or barely over half a dollar per day. To make matters worse, New Delhi has become very expensive.

Tragedies and untimely misfortunes, such as deaths in the family and illnesses, bring about major transformations in the lives of children and instil in them a sense of maturity and responsibility for the sake of the family. Their agency, in this case, is based on necessity. Children react to the situation by doing what they must—work for survival. Such work can be classified in the category of the worst forms of child labour. Agency in this case is not a free-floating agency—the child voluntarily and unconstrained by duress opting for a specific activity. It is the plight of the most deprived childhood.

There are stark contrasts between the lives of child labourers in rural areas and those who live in cities such as Hyderabad and New Delhi, but their agency under comparable family circumstances turns out to be fairly

---

Box 6.1 A Day in the Life of Iqbal

0700   Iqbal wakes up at around 0700. After washing his face, he goes to the public lavatory. Then he brushes his teeth and visits his friend Vijay. They take a walk and then go back to Vijay's house for a fifteen-minute session of a video game. He then rushes back home.

0800   Iqbal washes his clothes, takes a bath, and gets dressed. He then lights the stove and makes some tea. By then, his mother wakes up and begins washing the dishes. Iqbal helps her. He then serves the tea to the family and has some himself. Before leaving for work, he washes the cups and stacks them under the bed.

0915   Iqbal takes the bus to the workshop. The bus is very crowded but he pushes his way through. On the way, Iqbal excitedly points to a school building Kalkaji; that is the school he used to attend before the death of his father.

1015   After reaching the repair shop, Iqbal slips underneath a car and fiddles around with the machinery while lying on his back. After some time, his master Saheed asks him to assist him. Iqbal carefully observes Saheed who directs him to wipe the parts clean with petrol and then tightens the nuts and bolts. He serves tea to his master and has lunch at 1300. Until 1700 Iqbal and his two colleagues look into all kinds of problems, such as punctured tyres, discharged batteries, fused lights, malfunctioning gears, etc.

1700   As the boss leaves early, the boys too pack up at 1700. After waiting for about ten minutes at the bus stand, Iqbal boards the bus. At around 1815, after transferring onto another bus, Iqbal reaches home.

1815   On returning home, Iqbal changes into another set of clothes. He then chats with his mother. Then, he prepares tea. After having tea, Iqbal helps his mother prepare dinner by chopping, washing, and supplying her with whatever she requires. He also buys milk from the store. In the market, he bumps into some of his friends and chats with them.

2015   While waiting for his elder brother to return home from work, he watches cartoons on the television. Iqbal is in a happy and relaxed mood. For a change, he looks like a thirteen-year-old child. At 2030 the family has its dinner. Iqbal sleeps with his mother on the floor while his brother sleeps on the cot.

---

similar. Mahesh, who lives in an undeveloped district of Bihar (Eastern India), is a good example of a category of boys who at an early age (he is only twelve) shoulder the responsibility for the survival of their family. His family is steeped in stark poverty. It is in need of food, clothes, and shelter; the only property is a thatched-straw house. Mahesh says that he lost interest in everything after his mother died. He does not enjoy working in the fields, since the work is hard, the pay is low, and the landlord will never be satisfied:

> I am sweating under the harsh sun; there is nobody to see this. Everyone cares for money alone. He will try to pay Rs. 5 less when handing

Box 6.2 A Day in the Life of Mahesh

0600   Mahesh wakes up, goes to the toilet and then brushes his teeth with a bamboo stick. He rinses his mouth and washes his hands.

0700   He sits on the edge of a pond near his house. He is wearing a vest and a *lungi* (a wraparound for males to cover the lower portion of the body). He is called by the landlord to come and work in the field.

0800   He begins working with the spade. When he feels tired, he rests for a while and asks the landlord for *khaini* (chewing tobacco). After having *khaini*, the landlord goes home for breakfast and Mahesh goes back to work. Mahesh complains that no matter how much he works, the owners never appreciate. Mahesh is an honest worker. His body is oozing with sweat and the skin on his face tans. Mahesh resumes digging the earth until the landlord arrives with breakfast.

1200   Breakfast comprises four *roti* and a vegetable dish made of a local root. He takes the breakfast home and gives it to his sister. On the way, he says that he will be paid Rs. 20 for the day's work. On reaching home, he rests for some time and then goes to the hand pump to have a bath.

1230   Mahesh has a bath but does not use soap; he washes his clothes, puts on a T-shirt and pants and tells his sister to bring him his lunch, which consists of *roti* and a vegetable dish.

1330   After lunch, Mahesh sits on the banks of the pond and plays with a deck of cards. At around 1500 the landlord comes looking for Mahesh and pays him Rs. 20. Then, a boy comes looking for Mahesh and they decide to go and visit the weekly market, which is at a distance of 2 km.

1530   Mahesh informs his sister about his visit. On the way, they share jokes and pleasantries. Mahesh buys 2 kg of rice at the rate of 6 Rs. /kg and some snacks worth Rs.1 for his sister. On their way back, Mahesh stops at a tea stall and enjoys a cup of tea with his friends. By 1830 he is back home. He gives the snacks to his sister and feels good to see her happy.

1830   He asks his sister to prepare dinner. He pulls out a pot, lights the fire, and cleans the rice. His father arrives with a bottle of sesame oil and a packet of salt. His sister cuts the vegetable and cooks it. The family then sits near the oil flame and has dinner.

2000   After dinner, Mahesh goes to bed, which is a mere grass mat. Before retiring for the night, his sister washes the pots and dishes.

out the wages, but he stretches us to the limit. The landlords are only concerned about themselves. They are never concerned about the difficulties we face in ploughing and tilling and hoeing under the harsh sun. Instead of some concern for us, they accuse us of not doing our best.

Although education has become more widespread in the rural areas, also among girls, we still found many instances of girls and boys who at a young age started participating in all forms of work in and around the household, so much so that they had to drop out of school or never even attended school. In one of the villages of Rajasthan (western India), we encountered

Lalita (thirteen). She is the eldest child in a family of small peasants. The land they own is insufficient to survive. The father in addition works as a wage labourer in the village and as a helper to a mason in the nearby town.

Box 6.3 Day 1 in the Life of Lalita

0600   Lalita wakes up at 6:00 a.m., washes herself and fetches water from the well at a distance of half a kilometre; it takes nearly an hour to finish two rounds. She then spends half an hour sweeping the courtyard, room, and veranda.

0745   She then has her bath in a corner of the courtyard. Her breakfast consists of *jowar roti, dal*, and chilli paste, which was prepared by her mother before she left for work.

0815   After washing the dishes, she sits outside her house with her friends.

0900   She carries 25 kg of wheat on her head to the flourmill. She returns within ten minutes and then takes water for the buffalo and two heifers to drink.

0930   Lalita and her sister Saroj lead the buffalo, two heifers, and three goats into the pasture for grazing. They walk for an hour to reach the grazing fields, which is near the land they own.

1030   Lalita leaves the buffalo and the heifers by themselves to graze and weeds the onion field. Her uncle and aunt are present in the field with their children. While weeding, she chats with them. She finishes the weeding in half an hour and then sits under the shade of a tree, watching the cattle and ensuring that they keep away from the fields. In the meantime, she eats lunch (*roti* and *dal*), which she had carried with her. She then switches the water pump on, and after a while, leads the cattle to the small tank to drink water.

1400   She heads for the well and washes a bundle of clothes that she had carried with her.

1430   She joins her relatives who are sitting on a cot under the tree. On her aunt's request, she looks after her cousin who is crawling on the cot.

1630   Lalita, her sister, and their relatives set off for home. They walk behind the cattle and each time the cattle stray into the fields, she makes a distinctive sound that makes the cattle fall back on track.

1730   She goes to the flourmill. She pays the flourmill owner and carries the flour on her head back home. Meanwhile, her sister, Saroj, has tied the cattle in the shed. Lalita fetches fodder that was stacked in one part of the shed. She breaks the firewood into small pieces and carries them up to the hearth. By now, her mother has returned from her work.

1900   For dinner, she prepares a meal of *jowar roti* and chilli paste. Her brother Ramniwas and sister Saroj are the first to be served. Then, Lalita and her mother eat after which Lalita clears up.

2000   Lalita spreads a quilt on the floor in their living room. Her brother Ramniwas and Saroj have already fallen asleep. She waits for her mother who has to wake up early and be punctual for work. Otherwise, the supervisor might refuse to engage her.

The mother also works as a wage labourer. Lalita has a younger brother and sister, both of whom attend school. Because her mother works elsewhere Lalita must perform all the household duties, including cooking, fetching water, dish washing, sweeping the house and the yard, tending to domestic animals, and some on-farm activities. Her activities were observed for two consecutive days during the festive month of October.

On the second day, Lalita, on waking up, sweeps the courtyard, makes three trips to the eighty-feet deep well to fetch water in pitchers, prepares a breakfast of *roti* and *dal* for her siblings and herself, and washes the dishes using sand and water. She then rests for a while with her sister Saroj on a bench near the gate. Some of their friends pass by and enquire if Lalita would be taking the cattle to the fields for grazing. Lalita answers that her younger sister Saroj would be escorting the goats but that the buffalo and the heifer would remain in the shed as Saroj may not be able to manage all of them together. She also tells her friends that she has a lot of duties around the house that day on account of the festival of Navratri. She then makes her way to the cattle shed, carries a handful of dung, mixes it with water and starts smearing the courtyard with the dung paste. She finishes this work by 11:00 a.m., after which she bathes and washes her clothes. She goes to fetch water again at the hand pump, but since the queue is too long, she decides to go to the well instead. She makes two trips and refills the container of water kept for the buffalo.

After lunch, Lalita's aunt drops by. After she leaves, Lalita goes to sleep for an hour. On waking up, she makes two trips to the well to fetch water. At 5:30 p.m., when her mother returns from work, they begin preparing a meal of *churma* (flour fried with *ghee* and sweetened with sugar) and *dal*. Lalita makes approximately eight balls of *churma* and carries them to the temple as offerings for the deity. After prayers, she visits a neighbour's house and presents them with *churma*. After dinner with her family, Lalita goes to her maternal uncle's house to watch television. She likes watching *Ramayana* and other mythological shows. The news programmes do not interest her. By 8:45 p.m., she returns home, spreads a quilt on the floor of the living room and goes to sleep. At the age of thirteen, she has clearly established that she can live the life of an adult, working and managing the household and the cattle, and she is a good illustration of the premise, as defended by some child rights' activists, that children need not be constrained in a childhood of education and play only. But Lalita, after all, is a child and would not be living this life of hard work and unrelenting responsibilities if she had not been born in a poor family in a poor district in a poor country. Her agency is born out of coercion, not out of free choice.

Girls are involved in all kinds of activities around the household. In some cases, these activities grow into a major responsibility and allow the parents to go and earn income. Some girls at an early age go and work as agricultural labourers, like Mahesh in the earlier story on Bihar. In another village of Rajasthan in India, we followed Matra. She is the twelve-year-old daughter and youngest child of Chotu Ramdev and Prabhati, who have two daughters, two sons, a daughter-in-law, a grandson, and a granddaughter. Both the daughters were recently married to two brothers in another household and Matra will move to that in-laws' house in three years' time. She wears a wristwatch and a silver anklet. 'Her in-laws gave her those ornaments', her mother said with a smile. The household is a two-room house built under a government scheme for the benefit of the lowest castes. Chotu and his four brothers have twenty bigha of land and a well, which is now being deepened in order to solve the water problem. This year, they have not been able to grow anything due to the water scarcity. The parents, the sons, as well as the daughter-in-law Shivraj, are casual nonagricultural workers. Nowadays it is difficult to find work in the village, and they often have to go into town to work.

For two months Matra used to attend the night school run by an NGO, but when the school moved to the Bagaria cluster, Matra dropped out. Her mother says that Matra cannot attend the school now since it is at 'a far away place' (i.e., 1/2 kilometre) and it is not safe to send a daughter to school late at night. Matra can count money and is somewhat literate thanks to the two months at night school. Matra does household chores like fetching water, fetching firewood, preparation of food, etc. When the work is available, she also carries out wage labour in the village. Since there have been no rains recently, fields are lying fallow and presently there is no question of work in the village.

The next day Matra gets up at 0530. After having tea, she goes to the well to fetch water and finishes her bath by seven o'clock. After preparing her breakfast, she starts her journey to the worksite. Unfortunately, after reaching the worksite, the supervisor tells them that since there is not much work, they can go back home. On reaching home, she finds out that her sister Surti has come from the in-laws' house. The two sisters embrace each other and they talk for half an hour. Matra then goes to the well to fetch water. After fetching water, the two sisters talk for a while about the in-laws' house. After a while Matra brings a cloth and does some hand sewing. Surti mixes cow dung with water and smears the veranda with the cow dung paste. Meanwhile, Matra's mother grinds the red dry chilli to make a paste. At around 1100 both the sisters go to the neighbour's place. Around one o'clock Matra's mother calls the sisters to come home and have their lunch. After lunch and the midday rest, Matra goes to the well to fetch water, sixty litres in three rounds. She goes to the bathroom, has her bath but does not change her dress. She then sweeps the courtyard, starting with the area where the goats are tied. Meanwhile, Surti prepares tea, which they then drink together.

The two sisters sit on the veranda for half an hour and by 1900 they start preparing for dinner (*roti* and lentil). They first serve food to their brother Nandlal and father Chotu. Nandlal and Chotu hold plates in their hands on which *roti* and curry is served. They keep the plates on the veranda and

Box 6.4 A Day in the Life of Matra

0600	Matra gets up at 6:00 a.m. and soon thereafter goes to the well, at a distance of three hundred metres. Water is at a depth of 90 ft. She draws the buckets thrice to fill her pitchers. She carries the pitchers on her head, one of fifteen litres and another of five litres, the small one placed on the bigger one. She goes for a second round and a third round, and thus collects sixty litres of water.
0630	She sweeps the courtyard and starts kneading the flour for breakfast, before her sister-in-law takes over. She then has her bath in a makeshift bathroom located in a corner of the courtyard, and puts on fresh clothes.
0715	Matra packs her breakfast (*roti* and chilli paste) prepared by her sister-in-law and takes a spade and a pan with her. She goes to work in *feman* (the drought relief work organised by the village council), which is 4 km away. Together with some of her friends, they reach work around 0800.
0800	The supervisor tells them and around twenty other women what to do. The council wants to construct a small embankment so as to store the rainwater. Matra and two of her friends work together. They have to dig a measured area and carry the earth to a boundary. Matra digs, Sampat collects the earth in the pan and Mamta carries it away. At 0930, they have half an hour's rest, during which time she eats some *roti*. After having her breakfast Mamta digs the earth, Sampat collects it in the pan, and Matra takes the pan to the embankment site. After every half an hour they have a ten minute rest and change positions.
1300	The women have their lunch (*roti* with chilli paste). After lunch Matra goes to drink water. She cleans her plate by rubbing it with sand. After lunch everyone rests for half an hour.
1400	Matra, Sampat, and Mamta finish the rest of the digging by 1530. Then they go to drink water once again and gossip with the women at the site. They talk about ornaments. They return to the worksite at around four o'clock to spread the earth evenly on the embankment. By 1645 the work is over and they start moving homewards.
1700	The girls walk home, and discuss the work to be done at home and how to organise things tomorrow morning so that they can leave on time.
1800	Reaching home she goes to the well to fetch water in two pitchers. She washes her feet and hands, and then goes to the neighbour's place to talk with their sister-in-law about the food that is going to be prepared in the evening. She returns and sweeps the courtyard.
1900	Matra prepares the food for dinner: *roti* and lentils. She kneads the flour, forms the *roti* cakes and bakes them.
2000	She sits down to dinner with her father and brother. After dinner Matra washes her brother's and father's utensils along with her own. She rubs the utensils with sand and washes them with water.
2030	Matra waits for her mother and sister-in-law to finish their dinner. She serves them *roti* and *dal* and gives them water to drink. She then brings the cot and the quilt to the courtyard and lies down to sleep.

wash their hands. Matra and Surti eat their food together. They hold the *roti* in their hands and curry on the plate, which was earlier used by their brother. Mother Prabhati uses the plate of her husband. By 2030 dinner is over. Surti washes the plates while Matra arranges the bed on the veranda. The two sisters and their mother will lie on the quilt while Chotu and Nandlal will sleep on the cot in the open courtyard. They soon fall asleep and will get up at 0445 in the morning. They shall have to get up that early since they have to go and fetch firewood 4 km away and this has to be done before daybreak so as to elude the forest department people who would confiscate their axes.

In the discussion on child labour, it is sometimes argued that child labour is part and parcel of the cultures of developing countries and that no foreign concept of a child-labour free childhood should be imposed on them. The cases of Matra, Lalita, Mahesh, Iqbal, and Shobha inform us that all-engrossing types of child labour are the exception rather than the rule. Most children go to school and do not do more work in and around the household than appropriate for the age. That is the dominant local culture and children who do have to work from early morning until late at night are paying the price for being born poor or for living in a family that has suffered tragic deprivation. In the debate on child labour, these children should clearly be set apart from the other children who indeed, within what is considered proper within their own culture, do some odd jobs here and there.

6.3. WHAT TYPE OF WORK?

The type of work children carry out depends on many factors. The most obvious differences are found between the urban and rural areas. In general, according to the statistics, there is more 'child labour' in rural areas than in urban areas. However, that was not the case in all research areas. The prevalence of child labour also depends on the particular opportunities in the labour market. The rather isolated rural villages, with hardly any economic dynamism or development of a monetised economy, offer fewer opportunities for (adult or child) labour. For example, Batie (Burkina Faso), a trading centre, offers relatively many opportunities for children to find a paid job. Of the eighty-four children in the Batie sample, thirty were working for an income and twenty-five were working at home; in the rural Dem, on the other hand, the figures were respectively sixteen and eighty-eight in a sample of 184 children.

In urban areas it is more common for the children to help with small business and street selling. In rural areas, children are usually involved with farming. For the purpose of assessing the work-participation pattern of children in rural areas, we have categorised all the types of jobs into three major categories:

- unpaid noneconomic family work, which includes work such as sibling care, food preparation, water fetching, cleaning of vessels, firewood collection, cleaning of house and yard, etc.
- unpaid economic family work, such as animal tending, fodder cutting, planting, on-farm activities, assisting other family members at shop/restaurant, garbage collection/storing, collection of cow dung, etc.
- wage work, which includes work as a domestic servant, shop/restaurant servant, attached labour, casual wage work in agriculture and nonagriculture, etc.

Whereas unpaid noneconomic work is done by children in all types of households, wage work tends to be limited to the poorer families. In table 6.1 we have used landholding as a proxy for poverty. The data of the two villages in Bihar, India, show that the phenomenon of child wage labour is largely limited to landless and marginal land owners. Overall, less than 10% of the children are involved in wage work; most of them belong to landless families. Around half the children are involved in family economic activities. The highest proportion of children involved in these activities are found among the small peasants group (less than one acre) followed by the middle peasants group (five to ten acres). Quite a number of these children, particularly in the middle peasant households, would also be going to school and would be involved in light types of work.

Many children, across the different research areas, have some experience with paid employment, either while attending school or after leaving school. As we saw in the previous section, financial compulsion is usually a compelling factor for children to participate in income-generating work. Children of rich or economically stable households have more time to learn and play.

This difference is illustrated by comparing the daily schedules of Julio and Ricardo, both from rural El Torno, Bolivia. Julio (fourteen) is from a

Table 6.1 Involvement of Children (%) by Type of Work (Bihar)

Owned land (acres)	Unpaid family work (noneconomic activity)	Unpaid family work (economic activity)	Wage work
Landless	79.7	43.8	15.6
0–1	89.9	64.6	5.1
1–2.5	94.0	36.0	0
2.5–5	68.4	57.9	0
5–10	50.0	60.0	0
>10	87.5	37.5	2.5
Total	84.0	51.5	9.1

relatively less deprived family and attends school in the afternoons. During the week, he sells drinks and candies to children attending the morning school. In the afternoon his sister, who attends the morning school, takes over his work. After the school day is over Julio often stays on the school playground where he plays football and hangs around with his friends. Julio only helps on the family land during the agricultural season and during the weekends. He has 'a lot of free time' in which he likes to play football and stroll around with his friends.

In comparison, Ricardo (fifteen), who attends the same school for the evening programme, gets up at 0630 and works on the land until 1700. Then he goes home, changes his clothes and goes to school. The land on which he works is one hour's walk from El Torno, which means he only just makes it on time to school. When he comes home, he still has to do his homework. During the agricultural off-season, he works 'in the river', getting stones and selling them to the local cement factory. The only free time he has, according to him, is 'at night when I am asleep' and on Sundays during the agricultural off-season.

The case of Ricardo was not an exception. In the study in Bolivia, respectively 84% and 68% of the evening school children in El Torno and Santa Cruz stated that they only rarely have free time (Moreno 2002, 168 and 107). The evening school was actually created to 'enable members of poor families to work during the day to complement the family income, and at the same time go to school' (director of the evening school *Mario Guzman Aspiazu* in El Alto). Our daily schedule data shows that whereas the children who attend the morning and day schools work four hours a day, the children who go to the evening schools work eight hours. Whereas the former need not necessarily be classified as child labourers, the latter definitely are working too many hours a day and cannot possible spend enough time on school and learning.

When they work as labourers, the children are vital for the survival of the family. Child labour then is not a subjective choice against other alternatives. Bonifacio (twelve) illustrates such a case. Bonifacio's father died two years ago in a car accident, and he and his brothers now live with their mother. He works in a *chaperia* (garage) because 'at home we need the money to eat and to send my brothers to day school'. After Bonifacio returns from the evening school, which takes him half an hour using public transport, he helps his mother with the household tasks: cooking, doing the dishes, and cleaning his room. There is no alternative he says, 'My mother also works and so she does not have the time to do all this. Who else will bring us the money? While my mum works, we all have to help in the house. Who will cook when my mum is working?' Another example of this heavy burden is the case of Javier (fourteen). On weekdays he works in a bicycle store in a local market in Cochabamba, and in the evenings he attends school. In the weekends he is with his father, a public bus driver, as an assistant selling the bus tickets. He says,

'If I do not help my dad, he will have to hire a helper. We cannot afford that. Of what money will we eat when I do not work? Who will pay my school expenses?'

Differences in labour participation are influenced by age. Working hours increase as the children get older. Table 6.2 shows the percentage of children participating in different types of work according to age in the Vietnam study. Older children are always more involved in all types of work. For work that is considered light, such as child care, the percentages of both age groups are rather similar. On the other hand, there is a big difference in the percentages of children involved in heavier work such as crop collection and working in the rice fields. In cash-generating jobs, such as shining shoes, inflating bicycle tyres, and so forth, the jobs are usually done by older children. This division suggests that parents by and large have a normative understanding of what work fits the child at a particular age and that they, unless circumstances compel them, will not expose the child to dangerous and physically exacting work.

Even though in some circumstances girls in Vietnam were found to have longer working hours, by and large boys and girls spend an equal amount of time and energy on household tasks. Whereas more girls than boys were involved in jobs like cooking, washing dishes, and cleaning the house, boys spent comparably more time in the field. This difference was

Table 6.2 Child Work Involvement by Age Group (% of Children, Vietnam Sample)

Type of work	9–12 years old	13–16 years old
Cooking, washing dishes, sweeping house	33.3	56.6
Harvesting crops	12.9	29.6
Working in rice fields	10.4	30.8
Tending buffalos, cows	14.2	23.6
Breeding pigs, poultry	8.2	27.0
Gathering firewood	11	18.2
Baby care	11.6	12.6
Fetching water	2.8	11.9
Husking, pounding rice	1.9	5.7
Independent trader	2.5	9.1
Assisting parents in trade activities	5.7	12.9
Self-employed (shoe shining, bicycle tyres, etc.)	1.9	8.5
Other work	6.9	6.6

less pronounced in urban areas. Table 6.3 shows the gender division of current child-labour patterns in rural Vietnam. The percentage of boys and girls involved in different types of work does not vary substantially. Surprisingly, there is no big difference in boys and girls participating in work said to be 'female oriented' such as sweeping the house, washing dishes, and cooking. Findings show that 43% of boys and 46% of girls undertake these tasks, while 16% of girls and 9% of boys have to take care of their younger brothers or sisters.

The differences in work involvement between boys and girls were more pronounced in the other countries of the study, especially in Latin America, where girls repeatedly complained about their workload in the household. The explanation which girls have for this gender division of work is *machismo*, which they say is maintained culturally as well as politically. Jessica (nine) for example stated, 'it's that the men here are *machistas:* they think that women are only good to help in the house, for nothing more. How can one change men? *Machismo* is so deeply rooted in them, it's just impossible.' Marisol (fifteen) also blames patriarchal structures, which are sustained by the political system. 'They (the politicians) do nothing about this *machismo*. It's that our government is bad, they only help the men, not the women'.

Many girls do protest against this gender division. One of the most common strategies is to argue with the parents. Benita is an example of this: 'Yes I have a lot of fights with my parents and sometimes I really want to run away. Why should I stay in the house helping all the time while

Table 6.3 Proportion of Child Work Involvement in Vietnam by Gender (%)

Type of work	Boys	Girls
Tending buffalos, cows	20.0	17.8
Breeding pigs, poultry	16.2	18.7
Baby care	8.9	15.6
Cooking, washing dishes, sweeping house	43.5	46.3
Gathering firewood	14.3	14.3
Fetching water	8.3	6.3
Working in rice fields	19.0	22.2
Husking, pounding rice	4.1	3.5
Trade activities	5.1	6.7
Assisting parents in trade activities	7.9	10.8
Self-employed jobs	5.4	5.1
Harvesting crops	20	22.5
Other work	6.0	7.3

my brothers can go out?' Another common strategy is to escape from the house (*escapar la casa*) whenever the parents tell them to help for an unfair amount of time. 'My parents are very strict. When I want to go out I have to ask a million years in advance. So I am just obliged to escape if I want to play and see my friends, while my parents prefer me to stay inside and help'. Another strategy is just to comply and to aim for a different future. Maribel (fifteen, also in Cochabamba) criticises the gender division that her own parents use:

> I am not going to make the same mistakes that my parents made in educating my brother. When my brother comes home, my mother tells me: child, go and serve him, go and do this and that. And this is not just. From childhood my parents taught me how to cook. But I think that the boys also should learn this. It should be equal, not that the girls should do everything, while the boys are in front of the television. I am not going to make this mistake while educating my children. I will make sure that my children do not grow up to be *machistas*, that they do the same things as women.

In Bolivia and Nicaragua, the number of boys 'working' was substantially higher than the number of girls 'working'. On the other hand, the percentage of girls 'helping' was higher than that of boys. The girls were usually found helping their mothers with household tasks like cooking, washing clothes and uniforms for their family members, doing the dishes, and so forth. Boys on the other hand usually help their fathers in their work outdoors. There are, however, some outdoor activities that are also performed by girls. In El Alto for example, it was common to find girls helping their mothers sell goods on the market. Statistical material shows that market activities are mostly limited to girls: in El Alto the percentage of women helping their mother selling on the market is 15% in comparison with 8% of the boys (Llamos and Moreno 2003, 39).

In the rural village of El Torno, however, gender differences are not that pronounced: 31% of the boys and 38% of the girls stated that they worked in agriculture (Llamos and Moreno 2003, 98). Therefore Moreno states that in the rural areas 'the economic participation of women, from children up to adult life, is similar to that of the men'. However, whereas 11% of the boys state that they help within the household, 25% of the girls claim to do the same (Moreno 2002, 143). But also in terms of helping in the household, differences in the countryside are less pronounced. Whereas in the city the difference between boys and girls 'helping' in household tasks is 18%, in the countryside the difference between girls and boys helping is only 8%. Actually, unlike what one would expect in a country known for its *machismo*, many boys in the rural areas were found 'helping' their mothers. In El Torno, unlike in the cities of El Alto and Cochabamba, we even met boys complaining that their sisters were not 'helping' enough:

I help my mother with everything, also in the evening. For a while I watch television and then, when it is time to cook, I help cooking, I peel potatoes, that is how I help. Sometimes I have words with my parents, because my sister does not want do anything. I have to do everything. I have to cook, and when she has to cook she just leaves to play. (Edgar, ten, El Torno)

Despite these examples of unusual gender roles, girls usually work more than boys. Some parents explained this gender division by saying that girls have to help within the household in preparation for their future. Most of the girls themselves, however, did not accept this gender-based judgment, as is illustrated by the words of Lyla in Cochabamba (fourteen):

There are some men who think that women only exist to serve in the household. The women are not allowed to leave for one moment. The men can leave; he can go to his work, go to drink, to wherever he wants, because he works and it is his money. In the meantime, the wife is in the house taking care of the children. I do not think that is good at all. One marries because one wants to form a family, when you marry you are not buying a housemaid! Women can do the same things as men. Like nowadays there are some women who maintain their husbands. So why are these men still *machista*?

6.4. THE CHILD'S ATTITUDE TO LABOUR: BOLIVIA AS A CASE

We have looked at the contribution of children to the household income and their actual participation in different types of work. Below is a discussion of their attitudes towards the work they perform.

Although children cannot normally choose the work they have to do, they have clear preferences for certain jobs. Children's dislikes for certain types of work provide an insight into their own criteria for categorising work. Children like to help and please their parents, to contribute to the family's income and well-being, and to earn money for their own education. They also like to do activities that are suited to their physical abilities. Children prefer to do work that allows them to have some fun or to pursue their personal interests at the same time. Boys tend to prefer social activities that allow them to be outside with their friends, while some girls show a preference for the quiet of their home where they can do their chores while pursuing their studies or play with their younger siblings.

Activities that children dislike are those which are hard and heavy, expose them to excessive heat or cold, are embarrassing or shameful, make them vulnerable to being scolded or physically punished, are dirty, uncomfortable, and pose risks of physical discomfort and injury. Some girls and boys also expressed an aversion for activities that are more commonly performed by the opposite sex.

The appreciation of the work they do appears to relate to a variety of factors, one of which is definitely the environment in which one works, particularly the contrast between work in the household and working for others. The Bolivian study serves well to illustrate this. When the children in Bolivia were asked what they thought of their working situation, most of the children responded positively. The investigation in Santa Cruz, El Torno, and Cochabamba led us to believe that respectively 30%, 56%, and 60% of the working children defined the work which they did as 'good' (Moreno 2002, 106 and 167; Llamos and Moreno 2003, 61). However, when the children were asked if they wanted their own children to work in the future, they all responded with a resounding 'no'. The words of Marina (fifteen), who was working herself as a cleaning maid, are illustrative:

> No I certainly do not want my children to work. That I am suffering myself does not imply that I want the same for my children. I do not want them to become like me: working all day. I want them to have a good education and become professionals.

The children who were not working also responded negatively to this question. Javier (twelve), who attends the day school in Cochabamba, said, 'No I do not want my children to work. They can help in the house, but only work full time when they have completed school'. These responses imply that, as opposed to their initial statements of liking their work and considering it as good and beneficial, the children do not really think that highly of their work. The positive appreciation of work is a consequence of the economic difficulties which they are in and since they hope for a better future for themselves, they would not expect their own children to work.

The children mentioned various reasons for disliking certain types of work. Many children mentioned the bad bargaining position which they have at their place of work. A weak bargaining position prevents them from standing up for better working conditions. This came into the open during the celebration of the International Labour Day in the evening school Simon Bolivar in Cochabamba. The aim of the celebration, the director of the school said, was 'to teach the children their rights and give them back their self-respect as workers, as they are often heavily underpaid and abused on the work floor'. Wilmer (fifteen), who works in a garage, held a brave speech in which he told the other working children: 'We should not let our bosses exploit us, just because we are children. We should stand up for our rights as children'. However, afterwards he confided that he himself was very sceptical about realising his wish: 'It is almost impossible to demand better working conditions for working children. We do not have syndicates. If we demand better conditions we will be fired, and then what? With what money will we eat and clothe ourselves?'

The following examples will more extensively illustrate some of the consequences of this weak bargaining position in relation to the necessity of working to supplement the family income. The majority of the working children earn only less than 10 Boliviano (3 Bs. = 1 euro) a day (Llamos and Moreno 2003, 41 and 57). The working children complained about their low wages, but at the same time thought it impossible to change because of their bad bargaining position. For example Bonifacio (thirteen), who works in a garage, is paid 5 Bs. a day:

> I have to work from seven in the morning to five in the afternoon. It is very hard and dirty work and I earn little money, but we need it anyway. I would like to have a better wage though. But how can I ask for this? My boss will just take another kid, there are many children looking for work. Other work is difficult to find.

Another example is Carmelo (ten), who works in a sewing atelier in El Alto from 0800 until 1700. He took a realistic position: 'My work is so boring and it hardly pays. But I have no choice really, there is no other work'. The need to work in combination with a bad bargaining position mostly leads to underpayment, but can also often lead to physical abuse on the work floor. For example, in El Torno 39% of the working children stated that they suffered abuse on the work floor; in Santa Cruz this percentage was as high as 39% for boys and 61% for girls (Moreno 2002, 87 and 151). There were multiple reports of girls being abused while at work. Benita (thirteen), attending the evening school in Cochabamba, told us:

> I was working, but it was horrible. I am not referring to the money, but my boss was treating me badly. He often screamed at me and beat me. But my family needs the money and it is difficult to get another job. So I just had to endure until I found other work.

The combination of economic necessity and a bad bargaining position can lead to some working situations being compared to slavery. When parents are not in the position to support them, a number of children live in with their bosses and have to comply with their wishes. An example is Maribel, whose mother could not pay for her upkeep and who now lives with another family where she cleans and cooks. Her working conditions are akin to slavery: 'Often I am not allowed to go outside the house compound. I am not even allowed to go and visit my mother. My boss tells me to stay and I have no other option but to stay. I cannot go back to my mother because she does not have the money for my upkeep.' Housemaids generally have great difficulty getting some time off for themselves. Thirteen-year-old Laura had to tell her principal that she would not be able to attend evening classes in school anymore: 'My boss does not want me to come to the evening school anymore. They themselves like to go out at night and I have to look after the children'. The director confirmed that 'in this way I lose some ten to fifteen children every year. Every time I propose that I go and talk to their bosses, but they do not want me to as they are afraid of losing their jobs. So the poverty of their families forces them to abandon their study'.

Bad working conditions in combination with a weak bargaining position can also lead to physical injuries. Bonifacio (thirteen) who, as stated earlier, works in a garage scrubbing the paint off cars, told us:

> I do not like my work at all. After a day of scrubbing, my whole body hurts. My back hurts from bending over all the time, my hands hurt because of the scrubbing, my throat hurts because of all the paint that comes off, and also my ears hurt because of that stupid scrubbing machine.

In El Alto many children work as a *voceador* (bus attendant). Their job is to call the destination out of an open window or door and they are thus exposed to drafts at all times. In the freezing temperatures of El Alto this job can have serious effects on the health of the children. During the study we met many *voceadores* who could often not attend classes because they were sick with fever or pharyngitis.

Many children complained about the health consequences of physically hard agricultural work in El Torno. Evadin (ten) said, 'Working on the land is hard work, you will be working hours in the burning sun, your whole body is hurting, especially your back, and then you have the danger of the snakes. I don't like working on the plot'. Ricardo (thirteen) is aware of the consequences: 'Because of all the agricultural work I do, my body will be burnt out by the time I am thirty, just like my uncle. Now already my back is hurting. That's why we in Bolivia use so much coca. Without coca we can not cope, working like this!'

Besides the physically harmful effects of work, the children also mentioned the psychological consequences of long working hours in harsh conditions, mainly due to the lack of love and affection. When a child works all day and goes to school in the evenings, little time is left for being with family. Children in the evening school often complained about working all day and studying in the evenings; they explained how they missed out on their family's attention. The need for a connection with the family was emphasised by Victor (twelve), who every day from 0800 to 1800 works as a metalworker in a garage in El Alto:

> My work sometimes makes me cry, all the time you are working, they will not let you go out to see your family or friends for one single moment. I am just sitting there all the time by myself. Therefore I am happy when I can leave for my house and visit my brothers and can see my mum.

Juan voiced his discontent by stating that he would never educate his children the same way as his parents did: 'I would never send my children out to work all day. That seems to me like amputating my own hand or my own foot. You need to be with your children, give them the love and affection they need.' In the same way, Marina speaks about having children: 'I would never send my children out to work. I want them to be with their parents. I want them to have the love and affection my parents never gave to me.' Missing out on the love and intimacy of the family indeed was one of the interesting features which the children mentioned as belonging to the direct and indirect effects of child labour. Childhood after all is the period in life that one spends with the family, in a protected and lovely environment.

6.5. LABOUR AND AGENCY

Despite their inability to bring about structural changes, children nevertheless employ various strategies to make their situations more bearable. The strategies usually offer no more than short-term breaks though. While the diverse strategies can be considered as a form of 'agency', this agency changes neither patriarchal culture nor economic structures. The children are incapable of permanently changing their environment and agency then works on an escape option.

Many children deliberately choose to work in an attempt to relieve their parents from economic pressures. This choice can be seen as agency, as it is indeed one way to change one's situation. However, being compelled to work because of one's economic and social situation should only be seen as a second-best option, and indeed children and parents alike are not satisfied with this form of agency. Children who feel obliged to continue performing work that they dislike eventually deploy various strategies to ease the strain.

One of these strategies has already been mentioned: escape. During the study we witnessed many children who had been sent to family relatives only to flee back to their parents again. Children can also complain about their situation to their parents, and at times this may bring about the desired effect. For example, Edgar (eleven), who lives in El Alto, was working as a metal worker. He had to work eleven hours a day, and considered his situation unbearable: 'I did not like my work one bit. I had to work so many hours, and they only let me pause for fifteen minutes. Then again they did not let me leave and see my friends. And it was very hard work'. Edgar repeatedly complained about his job to his mother, which in the end had effect: 'in the end my mother did not think it was worth it; they paid me so little'. Another example is Violeta (fourteen, evening school, El Torno). She was working as a baby-sitter and housecleaner. She told us how her boss beat her. 'When I told my dad he was furious, and took me out'. Marisol (twelve, Cochabamba): 'My dad does not want me to work anymore. I was working before, but my boss was treating me badly. He was screaming and often beat me. That's why my father does not want to send me working anymore'. These cases indicate that occasionally action is undertaken against exploitative forms of child labour, particularly when the treatment of the child is considered as inhumane and parents are in a position to intervene.

Another form of agency to escape negative forms of working was 'calling in sick'. David (eleven) works as a bus attendant and attends the evening school in El Alto. He gets up at 0630 and works until five in the afternoon, but he has an escape route: 'Sometimes when I am really fed up with my work, I call in sick for a day. Then I sleep late and pass the day walking around. In this way, I recharge myself. If I do not do this I would go crazy I think'. This form of resistance, even though it is only for one day, also shows the 'agency' of the children.

In some cases, children just escape to the streets and do not come back for a few days. Joining a gang is also a form of agency. According to Moreno, since children are working, the working place, which often is the street, has become the most important agent of socialisation. Regrettably this is a worrying situation: 'This makes that they are obliged to assimilate and reproduce the subculture of the streets' (Moreno 2002, 101). This subculture, according to Moreno, amounts to alcoholism, drug addiction, stealing, prostitution, and criminality. Even many of the working children that attend the evening school do assimilate and reproduce this subculture of the street. These children usually have a group of friends, a gang, and they live with them on the streets for a while. So did David (sixteen): 'I did not like the situation in my house. I always had to perform tasks I did not like and I did not feel that my parents cared. Therefore, I left. I had a friend, who helped me. We would just steal and live like that on the streets.'

One additional strategy to cope with work dissatisfaction is just to forget. This was the case with fifteen-year-old Pablo. Pablo is a shoe shiner who attends evening classes in El Alto. One evening he told me he was a member of the Tupac Katari gang, a gang who operates in the neighbourhood of *El 16 de Julio* in El Alto. Pablo told us that every evening after class, he and his gang go to a bar to 'get drunk'. He invited us to come along. When we were sitting in the bar and the kids were already pretty drunk, we asked them why they were drinking so much. Pablo told me: 'If you would live and work the way I do, you would also be drinking'.

CONCLUSION

This chapter has made the point that, in addressing the phenomena of child labour, one should differentiate between child labour on the one hand and children doing work suited to their age to help their families and to learn the working skills on the other hand. In the latter case, work can be an integral part of a healthy educational practice. Children themselves also make this distinction while referring to 'helping' and 'working'.

Children working in and around the household are a basic element of daily life in the countries we studied. This work is partly a consequence of 'need', a direct response to the awareness of family poverty or hardship. The children whom we talked to showed an awareness of the hardship suffered by their parents, an understanding apparent in their willingness to take on a greater responsibility in the activities in the household. The phenomena of children working can thus be seen as a form of agency: through their work, which involves their own volition, they help to ease the economic poverty of their families. For example, children whose families do not have enough money to pay for their school fees can work to pay their own way, thus enabling some of them the opportunity to education that otherwise would have been beyond their reach. Doing so allows them to break away from some social constraints.

Children have different ways to contribute to the household economy. One way is the direct financial contribution by engaging in wage labour or trade. Additionally, children contribute in an indirect way to the family income by performing various tasks, which allow their mothers and fathers to go and look for work outside the household. The type of work children carry out depends on many factors. The most obvious difference exists between the urban and rural areas. In rural areas more boys and girls do varied types of jobs, mainly in agriculture, and they spend more time carrying out these jobs. In urban areas on the other hand, the children more often have to help with small business, selling products in the streets. In both areas children have to do jobs like fetching water, washing clothes, helping with cooking, cleaning the house, and doing the dishes. Boys spend comparably more time on the fields and girls are more engaged in the household, but the gender division is far from strict.

When asked about their own attitude to work, the children made it clear that they like to help and please their parents and to contribute to the family well-being. But they do prefer work that allows them to have fun. In many cases, as also observed by Cindy Katz (2004), the work they did was often 'playful'. For boys, work usually means being in activities that allow them to be outside, in the streets or on the fields; girls show a preference for chores in which they combine work with playing and studying and looking after the siblings. They have a distinct opinion on what constitutes work and what constitutes labour. Labour is hard and heavy; it is embarrassing or shameful and exposes them to physical discomfort and ill-treatment.

An important aspect of child labour, as perceived by the children, was the uncomfortable environment, separated from the relative safe environment, which the family usually provides. Being devoid of love, affection, and attention was considered as a loathsome aspect of child labour. In preindustrial times, children usually worked in the company of their direct family members and were surrounded by such protection, although the work itself could be very taxing. Child labour today often means that the child is taken out of that environment and has to cope with an adult world, immature and unprotected. Participation in work, if any, is disliked if the child had to fend for himself or herself without the shelter and the concern of the beloved and protective adults.

7 Problems and Priorities in Development

How do children define their needs? How do children prioritise their needs? What are the views of children on the process of development and how do they see their futures? What strategies do children deploy to fulfil these needs and aspirations? These are just some of the questions that will be dealt with in this chapter.

When deciding what is important in their lives, children have to deal with the institutions of socialisation around them. The practice of these institutions is based on their opinion about children's well-being, which in turn is based on a combination of tradition, experience in child pedagogy, and the future they have in mind for the children. Views on this issue can differ. Even a seemingly straightforward concept such as 'the best interests of the child' (clause 3 in the Child Rights Convention) is open to polemic debates. Something that is considered beneficial to a child from one perspective can be deemed detrimental from another.

Such differences in opinion become apparent when children are asked for their point of view and particularly when children become involved in projects that use 'participation' as their methodology.

When asked, most of the children initially said that, because of insufficient knowledge, they did not think they could play a role in the development of their communities. Moreover, they said that adults would not talk to them about development issues or listen to them, because 'adults think we are too small. Because we are still young, adults think they cannot sit down with us to discuss. Adults don't think that children have good ideas.' This was said by a group of boys in Ifakara (Tanzania), but many children in other areas made similar statements. It proved difficult to talk to children about their ideas on development, and it became clear that children had previously never really been asked about their ideas, problems, and suggestions for improvement. Children are generally made to think that adults are right and wise and that they themselves are too small to contribute ideas or practical suggestions.

Asking the children to speak up themselves is cumbersome to start with, but once they start talking, it is not always clear whether the children are reproducing ideas which they have heard from the adults in society or whether they are articulating the untold small wishes of children directly. During the study we noticed that children, when feeling that we were prepared to seriously listen to their ideas, indeed started speaking about their visions and their complaints. Many started to understand that by explaining how they see the world and the problems around them, they could give adults a better understanding of the problems which they face. Adults, children felt, are not always in the position to totally grasp, identify, and express the problems children have to deal with.

There is a variety of problems that particularly affect children emotionally and that cause anxiety, sadness, discontent, and fears. Among the concerns in Nicaragua, we noticed a number of needs that children usually are unable to express to their parents:

- the success or the failure in school
- inability to communicate with the father because of his absence or his alcoholism, and the conflicts within the family
- working excessively in or outside the house
- limited living space in the house which compels children to go out into the streets and contributes to stress and personal conflicts
- bad means of transport, particularly for going to school
- ill-treatment by adults at home, at school, or in the streets

7.1. CHILDREN'S AWARENESS OF THEIR RIGHTS

With constant amendments and revisions, the legal systems in most countries have clearly affirmed the rights of the child. The laws have been modified so as to create institutions for the care, protection, and education of children. The countries in this study were quick to sign and ratify the International Convention on the Rights of the Child and have adapted their legal systems and policies accordingly. The mass media, authorities, and social organisations have regularly disseminated the content of this Convention to the public.

In Vietnam, on a much wider scale than in the other countries, we found that the awareness of child rights had spread far and wide. We found a high level of awareness of the two important documents, namely the International Convention on the Rights of the Child, and Vietnam's Law on the Protection, Care and Education of Children. Nearly half of the parents in the interview sample said they knew about one or both documents. They have come to know of the child rights' documents through TV programmes and over the radio or the public address systems of the communes in the rural areas. Surprisingly, more parents in the remote hilly areas in rural Thai Nguyen know about these two legal documents compared to those in Hanoi and Nam Ha. The number of children who were aware of the Convention and the Law was also high: 48% of the child interviewees said they knew about the International Convention on the Rights of the Child. Around 73% of the children said that they had received information on their rights through the mass media and around 23% were given the information at school. They (a group of girls in Phuc Xa and a group of boys in La Son) understood child rights as follows:

> The rights of the child? Yes, we heard about them on the TV. We are not taught at school, just listen to the TV. Children's rights mean children have the right to live, the right to be cared for, and the right to play.

> We know about the rights of the child through the textbook on civil education and through TV. The Law on the Protection of Children says that children have the right to be cared for, that children are the country's future.

Although their understanding of the documents is somewhat superficial, they are a helpful reminder to them that they should be protected and be given care by parents, adults, and the government. The findings in Vietnam show that the children are conscious about their rights as children. They actively participate in family and social affairs and sometimes react against mechanical and orthodox ideas imposed on them by adults. Asked whether they had come up with proposals for changes in their family and community affairs, 40% said yes. The fairly high rate of active involvement is remarkable since the culture in Vietnam is influenced by Confucianism, which has a very strict and hierarchical social structure. It is an ideology which in a number of respects is akin to the machismo and adultism as described in the cases of Bolivia and Nicaragua. Under Confucianism, women and children are the inferiors who should be educated. They have no right to discuss or decide upon important family affairs, even relating to their own futures.

Since awareness of child rights has been improved recently, some local governments and schools have started involving children in the consultation process regarding plans and programmes that relate to them. For example, children are aware of the programmes launched by local governments and schools to keep the environment green and clean. The so-called teams of Young Advocates hold meetings to plan these activities. A group of schoolboys in La Son told us: 'We took the initiative. We enjoyed doing it so much. Our villagers also respect us. Everybody praised us'. Local governments have built houses for poor families, and children in the community are being allotted tasks to help in the household and to take care of patients or collect clothes, books, and notebooks to donate to those families. On this matter, Nguyen Van T. in Quang Son village commented: 'My school is carrying out some activities of collecting wastepaper and metal. The money from that collection is used to distribute to the families which were seriously affected by floods. I saw children on the TV who had died or who had to stop studying; I am very sorry for that. We should do something about it.' Some other children had the following activities to report:

> I also joined in the activity to support Cuba. I volunteer to reduce my little fund of pocket money for breakfast to contribute together with my friends. (Tran Thi Th in Phuc Xa)

> My house is next to H. H and his two brothers are disabled children. It is very difficult for three of them to go to school. Sometimes, I ask X and K to visit H's family to cook for him in order to save his time to study. (Pham Thi V., La Son town)

> We like to take part in programmes that support people in need. We sometimes face difficulties, too. That is why we understand their needs. (a group of female students in La Son commune)

These activities come close to involving agency (*chungse*) whereby children themselves develop initiatives, albeit within a format that has been provided by the adults. Around half of the children in the Vietnam sample took part in such activities. Doing public service and helping disadvantaged families are activities that may have been initiated by the adults but that are highly educational for children. These activities help improve their feelings of responsibility to the community and to care for others who have suffered bad luck. It is considered an appropriate way of forming the child's character and of developing a sense of social responsibility. The children have actively responded to this work and have made proposals and discussed them with the people in charge. The activities may not score very high on the participation ladder of Hart, which we referred to in Chapter 1 and which many participation-oriented organisations adhere to. Whereas for them, participation amounts to an autonomous position of the child in the world, for example organising their own village council and taking development initiatives, the children which were activated to live with *chungse* or agency were doing so in a development process and within institutions conceived and run by adults.

7.2. SPEAKING OUT

In other countries, the awareness of child rights and, even more so, its application in a pedagogical sense, were less developed. Children had ideas for their future life, but they often were at odds with the traditional socialisation of children, which tends to control children at all levels. For example, in Burkina Faso, the children, irrespective of gender, ethnicity, or age, made it clear that they feel subordinate to adults (mainly parents and teachers). Charles (fourteen, Batie) said, 'Early in your life you are required to respect anyone older than you, you are not suppose to show any kind of disagreement or resistance because otherwise you are labelled as 'impolite boy' and your parents will be scorned by the community'. Adama, a fifteen-year-old girl from Batie, was asked whether her family allows her to plan for herself and allows her to move freely. She responded angrily:

> I do not understand my parents; sometimes they treat me as if I'm a small girl or illiterate. In everything I want to do they interfere. I'm just fed up of that. I'm grown up now, and I'm aware of everything. I should be allowed to go where I want as long as it is safe and do with my time what I want to do, but I am not allowed to do anything.

Some of these children found it unacceptable that they are routinely disbelieved and regarded as morally incompetent. Yet at the same time they take on considerable responsibilities, e.g., in child care, household jobs, etc. It is a world in which children are very much part of practically all the activities going on in the household, not separated by generational work divisions, and yet are not seen as having ideas on what should be done and how it should be done. Children also reported being humiliated by adults, instead of the adults acting as good role models. The children talked about how they are not consulted, either at home or at school. Participation, like caring and respect, is a fundamental human need but the children usually feel that they have no say in what is going on around them. A group of pupils in Batie High School said bitterly:

> Whether at home or at school, you just see things happening, nobody asks you about your opinion, and you are not suppose to ask questions; they always say it is for your benefit 'we are doing it for you and not for us'. The teachers keep saying this to us, but we feel we should know at least what is going on.

For obvious reasons, children in different countries and in different regions (e.g., urban and rural) are likely to have different levels of understanding social problems. However, this study also found common features. A common aspect, which cropped up in all the countries, although less in India, was the concern with dangers involved with sex and drugs. Most of the children were aware that the use of drugs is harmful and they were determined to stay away from such social evils. In Vietnam, for example, almost 10% of the child interviewees, mostly in Hanoi, answered that they had seen one or more of their friends (schoolmates or neighbours) inhale, smoke, or inject drugs. Around 90% of the child interviewees in Vietnam had heard about HIV/AIDS and knew about its dangers. Some parents in Phuc Xa said, 'the children understand more of HIV than their parents. They know about it through TV. Currently, the mass media talks about it all day long.'

In Tanzania also, we were quite surprised to see how many kids had heard about AIDS and how relatively well informed they were, considering the fact, as they mentioned, of not being able to talk about sex, AIDS, and related topics with their parents and other adults. They gained information about HIV/AIDS through television, radio, newspapers, and pamphlets, and they informed each other; the older children had mostly learned about AIDS at school. The majority of our interviewees in Tanzania, also the younger children, were knowledgeable about the ways of transmission and prevention of HIV/AIDS. They knew about the dangers, as a group of children in Ifakara said: 'There are a lot of men who are suffering from the disease and they are trying to approach young girls. They give money and other nice things to girls. What is important is for girls to refuse these things, otherwise they will get it as well'. Most of the children were quite knowledgeable about the disease. Some of the girls especially seemed to have quite a good risk perception, linking the disease with the problem of schoolgirls having older 'boyfriends' or being 'approached' by men. Children in general said they should stay away from 'bad influences' like the street gangs, discos, drunken men, and dirty magazines and should focus on studies instead. A thirteen-year-old girl in rural Mwanza told us the following story about how one could get AIDS:

> If a man is too drunk, it is easier for him to get HIV. If he is drunk his mind drives him to have sex, he can convince the woman to have sex with him. Sometimes when a man is drunk, he can easily get persuaded to rape a woman. It is likely for someone who is drunk to forget using a condom.

The children, with whom we talked about AIDS, thought that parents were less concerned about the disease, for they said: 'When we try to talk about this, our parents don't think these issues are very important'. Usually, the younger children we interviewed knew virtually nothing about AIDS. They had heard 'things' on the radio, but could not tell us what it meant. A few had tried to ask their parents about it, but got beaten for their inquiry. They did not understand the reason why their parents beat them and they said: 'If you ask adults about AIDS they will just beat you. So you don't ask again. Adults think we are too young to ask about AIDS. We don't know why.'

Children are generally aware of social problems, and they came up with many suggestions for improvements regarding development issues, especially regarding those matters that concerned them. During the discussions, the children in Burkina Faso, Tanzania, and India, when asked about the major problems they faced, like the adults, usually started complaining about the lack of health services and schools, the prevalence of diseases, the lack of school materials, about poor transportation and infrastructure, the lack of water and food, bad quality of houses and sanitation, poverty in general, and problems related to the work of their parents.

Consciousness of the world around them obviously is a consciousness that is derived from the discourse of the adults around them, but it is also prioritised with the needs with which they as children are being confronted. Those needs are different from the needs of adults and listening to the children about their needs would be an essential element of a consultation process when preparing new development projects. The next few pages will discuss these issues.

7.3. HYGIENE, WATER, FOOD, AND CRIME

The field material drawn from Tanzania shows that children, when compared to the adults, were more concerned about disease causation and transmission. This included concerns about the environment, safe water, waste disposal, garbage, good housing, and sanitation. Children repeatedly said that 'people are suffering from diseases because our surroundings are very dirty with garbage around everywhere', and that since there are no toilets 'people are defecating in the streets'. The children told us that, especially during the rainy season, there are floods and the toilets become blocked: 'all the dirt and defecation streams through the streets, and we start suffering from diarrhoea and cholera because of a lack of toilets.' They complained about the smell, the flies, and the hazards the dirty environment causes to their health and complained that the adults do not care as much about the environment as the children do.

For adults, the space in which they move has a meaning different from how children experience it. People do dump their garbage everywhere, especially in open areas, which are often used by children to play games or sports. A group of children said: 'Parents do not play in the streets like we do and they don't want to walk far to dump their garbage. When we play or meet with friends, we are in the streets and we can smell and see the dirt, especially when people are urinating and defecating in the streets.'

Most of the children in the sample in Tanzania were school-going children. Since primary school students are taught about hygiene and disease transmission, they may have become more knowledgeable about health hazards than most parents, who may never have gone to school or, if they did, may not have been taught on these issues. This might explain the difference in the concerns expressed by the children and adults.

Like the adults in their communities, many children complained about the problems related to water. Not only about the quality of the water and the health consequences, but also about the lack of water. Children actually complained more than adults, for good reasons. As the main water collectors, children have to cover long distances to water sources and stand in the long lines at the water sources every day. In Chapter 5, we have illustrated a day in the life of Heera (fourteen), the eldest of five daughters in a low-caste and landless household in Rajasthan, India. She attends the night school run by a local NGO associated with PLAN International. Apart from many other chores which Heera has, collecting different types of water from different wells engages her for almost three hours every day. It was not surprising that one of the major complaints indeed related to the water problem. One of the children in rural Dar es Salaam explained to us why the lack of water, and the long distance to water sources, creates a problem for children:

> In our village water is a big problem. Collecting water takes a lot of effort. That's why people who sell water, sell it at a high price. Many children do not come to school because they have to fetch water. Water wells are far away from our village. Our mothers tell us that we have to go to the wells and when we get there, there is a long queue and you have to wait for about one or two hours before getting water.

As mentioned earlier, hunger and the lack of food was brought up as a serious problem by children in many areas, especially in Burkina Faso, Tanzania, and India. Most of them linked the problem with the poverty in their villages, which was often explained as a result of unemployment and problems related to agriculture. The poverty which they lived in was an all-embracing concern and in each case it was surprising to know how well-informed children were about the economic difficulties and the technicalities of agriculture. A thirteen-year-old girl from rural Mwanza confirmed what others had also been saying, namely that lack of food is the main problem in the village:

> Almost everything needs to be changed in our village. Many people are unemployed, so they do not have enough money to support the family. They have to keep on selling small things and what they earn every day is spent on buying food and nothing else. Because of the lack of money of our parents, we do not get enough food at home.

The children are conscious of their poverty because poverty has a direct impact on their life. It involves the incapacity of their parents to afford proper schooling, good food, and a comfortable home. Children may not always relate their own poverty to the inequality in society and to the exploitative nature of the economic system. Such sensitivity, however, was obvious in villages where the class divide was visibly present. In the villages of Bihar, where poverty is almost as severe as in Burkina Faso but where some families are very rich and many families are very poor, children were intensively aware of the inequalities in society. For instance, Jyothi spoke about large bungalows and said: 'How lucky they are, living in big rooms, sleeping on beds'. Similarly, Rekha spoke about the well-cemented house of the higher castes in the next village. She pointed out that 'we also would like to have a house made of brick, painted walls, a lavatory and a path leading up to the house.' Children, who live in these bungalows, she felt, could eat chocolates and cakes. Similarly, for Saritha, a good life meant having sweets, mango pickle, lentils, mutton, ice cream, chocolates, fruits, etc., which were all so much more enjoyable than the coarse *roti* she had every day. She was aware that being rich meant living in spacious houses, having good food, wearing pretty dresses and, more importantly, having access to good education and a good job. Similarly, in Rajasthan, the following comments were noted. Imran said that rich people have jobs, property with land, and eat milk products and two, or even three, curries with *roti*. Heera said:

> Illiteracy is poverty. An illiterate is more often a poor man than a literate. A poor man has no source of income. Since a poor man has no income, he has less money to buy food, make a house, etc. A rich man has a good house, a vehicle, and a television. Their children can go to school. Their school has a good teacher. For me, there is only an evening school, when the teacher comes. They have lots to eat.

Many poor children indeed associated affluence with having lots of food to eat, like ice cream, chocolates, and fruit. For children, being rich also means living in good, sanitary conditions and not being surrounded by garbage and foul smells. Iqbal, who works as a helper in a garage in New Delhi, knows that he lives at the wrong side of society and that everything around him makes that visible. He pointed out that the site of the garage was not good since it was located next to garbage emanating foul smells. As a result 'customers do not stop here and even when they do, they do not stay for long. There are hardly any permanent customers because the people who own cars are rich and despise the foul smell and would never like to stop here unless it is extremely urgent'.

Poor children live in a different space, often without access to the other space. Poverty, according to the children, indeed also implies being discriminated against. Caste discrimination and class oppression are prevalent. Bhagwan, a vegetable seller, told us: 'The high castes prefer to buy vegetables from the non-untouchable castes rather than from a *chamar* or other persons from the untouchable castes'. Mahesh is quite emphatic about the oppressive relationship that his employer perpetuates: 'no matter how hard he works, the landlords never appreciate it and try to hand out Rs. 5 less when paying the wages.'

The children in India by and large appear to be acutely aware of their low class and social status. They feel very offended when derogatory language is used against them. This apparently happens often in school. The children revealed that some teachers abused them by saying: 'You slum dwellers, you stink', or at times chastised them by saying: 'Keep away from me, you are stinking'. Remarkably, however, the children themselves preferred not to think in caste and ethnic terms. Even though caste restrictions seem to be fading in cities, they continue to operate in the villages but do not seem to have had much impact on the social relations of the children amongst themselves. They seem to cherish the ideal of a world of equality. In the opinion of children living in caste-bound villages of Rajasthan and Bihar, the caste system wrongly differentiates and divides people. They consider all children as friends, irrespective of their caste although they realise that caste plays a role in village life. Some children are rich, and many children are poor, but all children should be treated on an equal footing. All children should have equal rights and should be treated equally and with dignity—this is the basic message given by the children in private discussions and in group discussions. The case study in India informed us that the children are acutely aware of the negative consequences of the caste system and that it creates artificial divisions among human beings.

7.4. THE FUTURE, IN THE EYES OF THE CHILDREN

Two girls in La Son, Vietnam, said: 'I wish most to have a well-off, happy, and harmonious family, in which brothers and sisters love, help, and take care of one another', and 'I also wish my villagers become prosperous and rich, and assist one another.' Tran Van T. (fifteen) has a kidney problem and has dropped out of school. He had this to say about his future: 'I wish that my mother's health would improve, my sister would recover from joint disease, and my kidney problem would improve. If I am healthy, I can work and take care of my mother and my sister so that my mother doesn't have to sell bread anymore.'

The discussions with the children made it clear that the aspirations and hopes for the future are very simple. When asked whether they are satisfied with their current living conditions, most of the school dropouts said 'No'. The schoolchildren said that their conditions were 'acceptable', but not many of them were satisfied. Most of the children find that their families are too poor and that poor living conditions prevent them from learning and playing. They generally aspire to possess and enjoy all those good things in life that their present family's economic status cannot permit. They therefore all wish that their parents would have stable jobs and incomes, and that their family becomes prosperous, harmonious, and happy.

School dropouts, for example a thirteen-year-old girl from La Son, are particularly negative about future prospects: 'There is nothing to do in the village and I only want to go away from home to find a job. I still don't know what I shall do later, anything will do'. Similarly, a sixteen-year-old boy dropout in La Son told us: 'I cannot find any jobs here, I only want to go to the city to find a job.' Whereas most of the dropouts wish to resume school if circumstances would permit, schoolchildren worry that they will have to quit school before completing their studies.

The hopes which they have are very specific; for example: 'I wish to have my house repaired and enlarged, to have a bed to sleep on, and that my father will get a job to have more income. I hope that my brothers, sisters, and I will continue going to school' (a fifteen-year-old schoolgirl in Phuc Xa). Many children also said they wanted to find a good job when they grow up to make a living and help their family. Ideal jobs for both boys and girls are teacher, doctor, singer, worker, scientist, and footballer. Many girls also want to become footballers. A number of children from Vietnam gave the following statements about their hopes for their futures:

> I saw on TV that there are wars and disasters in many places. So many people have died because of that. I wish that in the future we won't have terrible things like wars and disasters.

> I want to become a policeman to fight against crime and drugs. Crime and drugs are bad for society.

> I want to become a singer. I will sing songs to make people love each other more and stop fighting.

In Nicaragua children had similar hopes for their futures. They dreamt of becoming doctors, lawyers, engineers, teachers, nurses, drivers, firemen, and masons. The reasons for the choices were related to social motivations and reflected sensitivity to values of solidarity. When they expressed a desire to become a doctor or a lawyer, the motivation usually was not that it would allow them to have a life of wealth and luxury, but that it would allow them to be good for society and to correct the injustice around them:

- a doctor can cure illnesses
- a lawyer can help and defend the innocents
- a teacher can bring knowledge to the children
- a driver can earn money for his family and send his children to school

The majority of these children in Nicaragua (70%) were confident that, if they studied hard, they would be able to realise their dreams. They were clear that they definitely didn't want to become involved in violence, in robbing, in killing, in rowdy behaviour and in disrespect for the parents and such 'bad things' that are 'detrimental to the child'. These statements do reflect a sense of ethical and political correctness, but they are also likely to be typical for children who, given an environment of love and protection, believe in and hope for a harmonious future of equity and solidarity. The future is by and large looked at positively. Despite the poverty, they expect a better life, more chances for the poor people and less family-related problems.

But doubts remain whether society will change, and dreams and hopes do not black out the despondent feeling that things may not really change for the better, particularly for those, as it was suggested, who do not have a caring family, do not study well, and do not behave properly. The suggestions by the boys and girls indicate that they have a good sense of their cultural, economic, and social environment and the capacity and the insights that allow them to come forward with ideas for a better development with proper welfare not only for their family and their community, but for the country in general. In that sense, their proposals for improvement relate to the local level (playgrounds, healthcare centres, a bigger school, streetlights, drinkable water, police protection to counter criminality) as well as to the national level (reduction of poverty, employment generation, eradication of corruption, payment of just wages, support to the most needy). The latter aspect is indicative of the fact that children, considering their age, have a critical consciousness. Their understanding of affluence and poverty of course is shaped by their immediate life environment. The more radical the environment, and the more politicised the discourse around them, the more children also will conceive their own life and their future in terms of the injustice of society. Luzmaira (nine, La Paz) as a very young girl explained such injustice not in terms of economic forces (landlords, moneylenders, big companies, traders, etc.), but in terms of good people and bad people:

> My parents do not have so much money. Some people are even so poor that they have to live in the streets. They do not have the money to buy houses and clothes; sometimes they do not even have the money to buy themselves a dinner. They do not have any work; bad people do not want them to work.

Depending on their ages, children blamed different actors for the lack of jobs, and had differing ideas about what should be done about the problem. The youngest children were vague and used abstract concepts such as 'bad people'. Most of the older children, however, were unanimous: they all blamed the government for the poverty of their families and for poverty in general. The children criticised different aspects of the political system, but it was the politicians themselves who received most blame for being corrupt. Fifteen-year-old Gabriela, who attends the day school in El Torno, Bolivia, told us: 'It is that our politicians who have put all our taxes into their own pockets. They are the government and whatever they do, they are not put in prison. For themselves they buy nice clothes, nice cars, they can live nicely. In the meantime for us there is nothing, not even work to earn some money.' Maribel (fifteen, Cochabamba) expressed her frustrations about the corruption and the ignorance of the Bolivian government:

> It's that our own government has stolen our money and in the end has brought more poverty to Bolivia than before. They accommodate themselves well, but for us they do nothing: our parents are without work. Our politicians only make promises but they never accomplish

a thing. And they are so ignorant. Our mayor does not take good care of our cities. He likes to stay in his own neighbourhood where it is clean, quiet, where there are no problems. However, he never visits other places, he never lived how we live here and he never suffered like we suffer. Our mayor has told us he would come, but he never does. So he does not know our problems, how can he solve them?

Corruption and lack of knowledge are two factors used to explain the prevailing poverty, but more politically conscience children deliver more specific criticisms. For example Juan (fourteen, El Alto) emphasized the wave of privatisation in Bolivia as a major cause of their problems:

It is that our government has sold everything, and bit by bit it left Bolivia poorer. They say that Bolivia is a poor country. However according to me Bolivia is a poor country in arms and nuclear weapons, but concerning minerals Bolivia is not a poor country. The problem is that we have sold them to other countries. Our government has deprived us of our minerals so that there remains nothing for us.

In the same way Ricardo (fifteen) commented:

It's that there are so many foreigners that escape with our money, and who can ever get that money again? It would be better if the Bolivian people keep the minerals. They say that Bolivia is a rich country in gold, silver, and petrol. With that money we could build more roads, more schools. And to build more roads and schools they need more labourers, and in that way we could create more work, so that people would not die from hunger anymore.

In this view, the main reason why poverty prevails is the absence of job opportunities, resulting from privatisation. Such a direct critique of neoliberal policies was not uncommon among children in Bolivia and to an extent also in Nicaragua. Neoliberal policies, according to fifteen-year-old Ricardo from El Torno, who exhibited a remarkable knowledge of national and international politics, should be understood from an international perspective:

We should vote for a person who ends up with the poverty and who does not sell our minerals to foreign companies. But this does not suit the United States. And if we choose somebody who does not suit the United States they will come and kill that person like they did with El Che, or they mix in our elections. So in the end it does not matter whom we chose, the United States will make sure they will get the president they want anyway.

Nely (sixteen, attending the day school in Cochabamba) commented on why she thinks the Bolivian government (in the days before Morales came to power) is so dependent on the United States:

> What happens is that Bolivia does not have anything. We have sold everything and that left Bolivia poor: there is no work anywhere. Yes, we have sold everything to the United States. That's the truth. If Bolivia does not do what the United States tell them, of what money will we pay our enormous debt? They cannot pay it, we have such a great debt. So in reality we are the slaves of the United States.

In Nicaragua, like in Bolivia, knowledge of and opinions about national politics were widespread. The children were usually outspoken and were able to list a number of major problems, such as exploitation, poverty, drug addiction, and criminalisation, as sources of their insecurities. The following suggestions were among those given by the children, which reflect their active mental processes concerning poverty and the associated social ills:

- People should work together.
- The government should be more active for the poor and create jobs.
- Corruption needs to be attacked.
- All people should be given a chance to study.
- Decent salaries should be paid.
- People should be provided with all the necessities of life.

When asked what they would tell their president to do, they said: 'employment for our parents, facilities like roads, schools, and hospitals in the neighbourhoods.' These ideas reflect the radical ideological environment that some of these children live in. The knowledge of children pertaining to politics seemed to be exceptionally high in Bolivia and Nicaragua, very low in Burkina Faso and Tanzania, and fairly developed in India and Vietnam. In the various localities in India, quite a number of children knew the name of the political parties and local elected member of Parliament, and they were generally aware of certain political issues that affect their lives and the living conditions of their families. There was also disbelief and cynicism among the children with regard to local-level politics. Children agreed that political leaders should be honest, listen to the people, and must try to solve their problems. All these children could be forgiven for having naïve views of the real world, but they could also be considered the moral conscience of that world, providing a discourse to reflect on. They wish a better world and a political system with honest people defending the good and fighting the bad. They are aware that the forces of the good are not yet in command.

CONCLUSION

Three priorities were voiced repeatedly: the need to have basic needs satisfied, to be protected by family and adults, and above all, to receive the love of their families. The data on the various countries has indicated that particularly the first priority was generally not satisfied. Children and youth, with the exception of Vietnam, are growing up under precarious social and economic conditions, devoid of basic services: unemployment, bad housing conditions, malnutrition, bad hygienic conditions, limited public space, limited supply of clean water, bad educational facilities, no sports facilities, and particularly in some of the cities, delinquency and rampant psychosocial problems associated with alcoholism and drug addiction. Children identified these negative aspects in their environment and perceived them as real hindrances in their personal development and their well-being. Confronted with such problems, various proposals were made, such as:

- places for leisure time, such as a playground and a sports ground
- basic services such as a health centre, bigger schools, street lighting, drinking water
- police vigilance to clamp down on delinquency, violence, and addiction
- improving the school, with good teachers, books, and furniture

Verbal and physical maltreatment of children by adults was observed in all research localities. A majority of the children we interviewed spoke of maltreatment by the adults in their villages and quarters, including the adults of their families. In Nicaragua, for example, we observed that one-half of the children felt that they were respected and protected by the adults, but the other half complained of regular maltreatment.

This chapter has shown that children, if given the space and the confidence, are capable of articulating their needs and deploy various strategies to fulfil these needs. It is possibly not sufficiently realised that children are aware of the problems that surround them and their families. They for example know about the dangers associated with sex and drugs, although would never be able to talk with their parents on these issues. They also know of the poverty they live in and, depending on age and the political environment, they can also perceive the causes of their poverty. They know that the children of the rich people have a better life and have better prospects for the future and yet they themselves are still hopeful of their own future. The image which they have of the future is wishful thinking rather than a realistic acceptance of their place in society but that wishful thinking expresses their demand on the adult world. They know of the discrimination and the segregation, but they want to foster the image which they have of a harmonious world where people live in solidarity and justice.

8 Conclusion
Structural Constraints and Agency

This study has looked at conditions in some of the poorest countries of the world, countries with low gross national products and low human development indicators. Conditions of the children in these countries are a particular matter of concern and demand increased public attention and policy intervention. The commitment underlying the research was clearly that children, wherever in the world they happen to live, should not be exploited as child labourers and should have full-time access to well-functioning schools. It is what Basu and Van (1998, 422) have referred to as an acquired morality in society. With the acceptance of the Child Rights Convention by the UN in 1989 and its ratification by practically all governments in the world, that morality has been acquired by all nations and cultures in the world. It is therefore safe to accept that that childhood has a universal meaning, at least if the concept is unpacked from its environment-specific behavioural aspects.

The focus of the discussion and the enquiry should be on ways and means to improve conditions from the perspective of universal rights and a universal morality. Despite the many indicators of an intolerable state of affairs and a lack of improvement in many respects, there is, however, also a positive side to development. The governments of the countries in this study have signed the CRC and national legislation has been reframed accordingly. Measures are being taken, also against the background of the Millennium Development Goals, to provide education and good health to all. Various national programmes, often supported by international agencies, have helped to improve children's living standards; these programmes have included population and family planning, the elimination of social diseases, poverty-alleviation programmes, the prevention of HIV/AIDS, clean water and environmental hygiene, etc. Progress is tangible, although, as we have seen, rural areas in Burkina Faso and Tanzania, and to an extent also in India, are not doing particularly well.

Children have benefited directly. The number of children suffering from diseases and disabilities in most countries has been reduced remarkably and so have the levels of illiteracy. But, even though education and health policies have worked, they have worked insufficiently for many millions of children. The structures and the environments, in which those unlucky children are embedded, remain precarious. The neighbourhoods and communities in which these children live are precariously balanced at many levels, thus limiting agency:

- a lack of hygiene, aggravated by the lack of water;
- a lack of appropriate public services (especially those related to health, transport, and playing grounds) in addition to cramped housing conditions;
- social problems such as delinquency, vagrancy, and drugs;
- lack of access to good education: most schools do not have the necessary conditions to provide quality education; the buildings are in poor condition, hours of teaching are limited, facilities are deficient, didactic materials and textbooks are lacking, classrooms are overcrowded, hygienic conditions are dismal, sports facilities are scarce, etc.;
- cash-based economies, with high prices and rampant unemployment or underemployment at low wages, turn the lives of the parents, and often of the children as well, into a daily struggle for survival, which is one of the reasons why many children in countries like India and Burkina Faso remain excluded from the school system;
- the public construction of new ideologies, norms, and values; schools and parents are continuously in danger of being overtaken and sidelined by the mass media, which (with the exception of Vietnam and India) are inundated with mass entertaining (foreign) TV programmes, which propagate anti-values such as violence, consumerism, hyperindividualism, and sexism;
- consequently, children and adolescents, as well as adult family members, face difficulties in satisfying their basic needs with regard to health, hygiene, drinking water, transport, leisure and sports, and personal security.

Due to poverty, especially in families with many children and in single-parent households, younger family members have to contribute their time and energy to the running of the household and even to the income of the family. Conditions of poverty thus particularly affect children, who not only do not get sufficient nutrition, but who must go without school materials and proper clothes, who have neither suitable space nor time to complete their schoolwork, and who lack adult supervision and guidance in general.

Contributing to the household is something that most children like. They help because the activities are of a light nature. But by and large, it is just done; being engaged in all kinds of chores belongs to normal childhood in the areas which we researched. Working in and around the household is a basic element of daily life. This work is partly a consequence of 'need', a direct response to the awareness of family poverty or hardship. The children knew of the hardship and were willing to take on greater responsibilities. The attitude denotes the children's values of solidarity and responsibility to the household, which were acquired by them at an early age. Child labour and excessive work in the household, on the other hand, did not belong to normal childhood and were found only in conditions of extreme poverty, often in combination with defective family structures. Children like to combine work with fun and did not see it as a burden since it was usually done within a context of love and protection. The phenomena of children working, not of child labour, can in itself thus be seen as a form of agency: through their work they help to ease the economic poverty of their families and they relate closely to the social unit in which they live.

A proactive policy is needed to improve the circumstances. The concepts of agency and structure are two basic concepts in the discussion of policy. 'Agency' is at the core of the functionalist school, which holds that autonomous individuals make and remake social reality. On the other hand, the structuralists maintain that social beings organise their lives within the parameters of existing social, economic, cultural, and political structures, and that these structures have class, ethnic, age, and gender divisions which first have to be attenuated before agency can come into fruition.

The actual behaviour of children is the best evidence of individual energy and vision. They all act differently in one way or the other. Agency is involved in each case, whether it is agency to bring about change or agency to make the most of existing conditions. Yet, despite the fact that different individuals living within similar environments act independently and follow a different course of action, this study has illustrated how the structural constraints continue to have an overriding effect. We observed how differences in children result in diverse actions. The individual child takes in its environment, assesses the possibilities (with a large measure of idealism and perhaps some measure of realism as well), makes a decision, and thus acts in the world. Because of the short period of the study in each area and the large number of children to be observed, it was not possible to examine these traits in detail. However, discussions with teachers and with children, in combination with the observations, gave a good indication that the children we met have a clear vision of life and function in their social environments as active subjects.

Some of this acting is performed under adverse circumstances, and children again and again have established their great potential as active contributors to the family and to social life. Resilience, rather than agency, may be the right concept to describe a set of qualities that foster a process of successful adaptation and transformation, despite risk and adversity. Feeny and Boyden (2004, 51) talk of biases and myths that plague our understandings of and responses to child poverty. These biases, they argue, arise as a consequence of conceptualising children as passive 'victims' while in reality, children and adolescents have a good understanding of the factors affecting their environment. This knowledge determines what they can and cannot do, but "this potentially valuable contribution is left untapped and ignored by families, development agencies and governments alike. The vast majority of literature on child poverty thus depicts it as necessitating a universal 'rescue and rehabilitation' response, rather than a more culturally sensitive and nuanced analysis of how children can participate in overcoming poverty". Observing the fact—poor children living in extreme duress exhibit resilience and agency—runs the danger of turning it into a general strategy for dealing with the most wretched children of the earth. The children are called upon to speak up and come with their solutions to poverty and misery. The responsibility is put on the children and the duty-based policy of rescuing and aiding these children may disappear in the background. Feeny and Boyden (2004, 52) actually warn against a romantic notion: 'Incorporating children in this way should not, however, exclude analysis of the larger social structure, for children are deeply embedded within important and influential networks of social, cultural, economic and political relationships'. Should the main focus of child-centred organisations then not be directed at the surrounding structures rather than at organising the children to participate and organise their own defence?

The introduction of the concept of child rights and of the participation of children in claiming such rights has contributed to the spread of the idea of children as subjects in their own right. It has become common for child-centred organisations to involve children in the planning and executing of programmes, more or less at the highest rungs of the ladder as Hart (1997, 41) had conceived it. Children are conceived as mature and responsible subjects who have to come forward with their own insights and solutions. Some organisations, particularly Save the Children and organisations working with child labourers (Swift 1998; Miljeteig 2000; Liebel et al. 2001; Cussianovich 2002; Liebel 2004), have taken an extreme position in claiming that young children are capable of working and forming their own union to defend their rights. The discourse on child participation has shifted to promoting children as agents of change or as agents for change and that projects should not be for and with children but by children. Children are supposed to start and run organisations that look after their interests, based on their own research and with adults functioning only as facilitators.

The ground reality is different, however (see van den Berge 2007a and 2007b; Roschanski 2007; and Nimbona and Lieten 2007 for a study of the child trade union claims). With the exception of some young adolescents in Bolivia, we have not met any child which could live up to the expectation of being a mature and respected partner in discussions on PRSPs, national development plans, school systems, debt-repayment schedules, or whatsoever issue with a direct effect on children indeed but for which children could not possibly have and should not possibly have a responsibility to bear. 'Child-centeredness' is an excellent point of departure, for as Hart and others have argued with so many words, a more mature cognitive development can be stimulated through dialogue and joint action with the children: 'the better we can understand the processes by which children are trying themselves to develop, the more we shall be able to become useful partners in this development' (Johnson 1998, 31). But the approach unfortunately also assumes that children have an innate knowledge and innate capacity to develop. They are considered a 'citizen' like other citizens, albeit with marginalised powers since adults are accused of not having allowed children to come forward as autonomous subjects. The broader objective of child-centred programmes based on such participation therefore is to include children's voices and participation in all stages of programming, as a standard practice in the community-development processes. This entails extending child participation to the analysis, project design, implementation, and monitoring stages of the programs. Enabling children to participate in all phases of programming is seen as the best way to ensure that working with children is child centred. Some see this as the 'the missing component'.

'Participation' thus appears to be a construction by child rights' ideologues and by some child-centred organisations. It is being applied through extension workers within their projects, and children in those projects indeed are coached to internalize the language of participation. In all areas which were studied in this research, participation in the eyes of the children had entirely different meanings: to be listened to and to have access to the mainstream infrastructure and institutions such as schools, sanitation, proper housing, a proper income for the parents, etc.

UNICEF has rightly asked the question whether in a world in which even so many adults are denied the opportunity to participate fully in society—exclusion, marginalisation, and alienation are some of the concepts used—encouraging participation by children isn't a step too far. Would the focus on providing a comprehensive educational and health infrastructure not have to relegate 'participation' to second position? The qualification which UNICEF gives to the concept of participation is fairly convincing. A child whose active engagement with the world has been encouraged from the outset will be a child 'with the competencies to develop through early childhood, respond to educational opportunities and move into adolescence with confidence, assertiveness and the capacities to contribute to democratic dialogue and practices within the home, school, community and country' (UNICEF 2003, 19). The exercise of agency and responsible citizenship is not something that is suddenly given at adolescence but is a faculty that is being shaped as the child engages with the world. The child should be stimulated to do this with a sense of responsibility and respect. When there is authentic child participation in the family, school, community, and society, 'we hear children and young people tell us that they are more confident in themselves, more aware of their community and its problems, more committed to serving and working with others and more optimistic about the future and their role in it'' (UNICEF 2003, 24).

The important fallout of participation in this sense is beyond dispute. Encouraging children to participate intellectually in development has the advantage of making children aware of developmental problems. That helps them to understand society around them and feel involved in what is going on. When they are conscious of community issues, they could possibly overcome alienation and may mature into adults who are more motivated, confident, and capable to be involved in public issues and community development. Making them understand the world today and preparing them for the future in fact appears to be a better child-centred policy than to coach children to become agents of change during their childhood days themselves, unless of course very exceptional circumstances demand them to do so.

Nevertheless, children could be more actively involved in phenomena which directly concern them. Improving public health would be one of the possible positive implications of children's involvement in development. Children who had been in school have clearly shown that they have knowledge and insight in disease causation, transmission, and prevention. Helping the children so that they are more able to apply their insight at a young age can result in significant and enduring gains in public health. To tap into the potential of children as actors, it is important to teach them that they have an individual role to play. By fostering this confidence in young children, they will develop into proactive, empowered adults who believe that change is possible. For this to happen, it is necessary for adults to listen and to encourage the children to articulate their ideas and concerns. The relationships between children and parents that we observed were generally loving, cooperative, and respectful. Parents desire the best for their children but do not have the habit of listening to the children and discussing with them phenomenon which are assumed to be the terrain of adults (sex, politics, poverty and exploitation, etc.).

Many children needed to be encouraged to express their own opinions, to critically think about problems and the causes underlying the problems. It became clear that for many children this was the first time anybody had asked them for their opinions. The degree to which they managed to participate in the conversations and discussions, and the amount of encouragement needed to make them participate, depended upon factors like the age and gender of the child, level of education and environment, but also on personal characteristics like intelligence and self-confidence. Children were knowledgeable of the world around them and apparently knew much more than their initial silence to our queries suggested. Particularly children in rural communities were more exposed to and involved in the world of adults around them, compared to the urban children.

This should be an essential lesson to implement: children have insights and also have anxieties, hopes, and frustrations and they should be listened to. That would be the first step towards meaningful participation. We have concluded earlier that listening to the voices of the children is an important aspect of child participation. It is probably more important than 'participation' as such, which is often considered to include having a say in all stages of programming and implementation of an NGO-run project. A child-centred approach stands to benefit from a child's vision of the world and throughout these pages, it has become obvious that children by and large are commanded and reprimanded; they are hardly ever listened to.

Children have their priorities, their view of the future, their worldview, their assessment of institutions and events. Knowing this vision and learning how to tap it for the better development of the child and the community are mandatory. To tap that knowledge is one thing, to put the child in the driving seat is a different thing. Judith Ennew (in Johnson et al. 1998, xviii) argues that 'muted groups, such as women, children, prisoners and ethnic minorities are unable to express their realities in ways that are acceptable to the dominant groups'. This power imbalance is sought to be corrected by Ennew not by some token involvement of the marginalised groups, which includes children, but by full participation. The question of child-centred (or women-centred) development intervention thus is 'how to incorporate their specific needs and views into decision making processes within the context of what is possible institutionally and culturally.' Ennew suggests on the one hand that their should be 'full participation' in the sense that children should get involved in 'decision making processes', but on the other hand reminds us that the context is a constraining factor. More thought should be given to the very essence of the child as a constraining factor (see e.g., Purdy 1992).

The vision of the child in poor neighbourhoods, without any shadow of doubt, starts with education as the first and foremost requirement to be fulfilled. In Vietnam, and to a lesser extent in Nicaragua and in Bolivia, and in the cities of India and Tanzania, primary education is accessible to all. However, education that stops at the age of eleven, as is the case in many areas, robs the children of what is a necessary minimum requirement for life in mainstream society. It is an essential requirement, not just for its career benefits, if any, but also for its socialising attributes and for the enhanced knowledgeability of the world.

The application of the rights of the child for many children is constrained by the environment they live in. The oppressive structures, which they live in and which many children could identify, are crucial when deciding on how best to provide 'protection' to children. The sociostructural environment in a child-centred approach is sometimes taken as a neutral ground, or at least as outside the intervention for change. The efforts to enable deprived children, their families and their communities to get mainstreamed into the development process, presuppose a level playing field. Since such a level playing field is absent in practically all areas, with conditions in Vietnam somewhat different, children by and large will have severely curtailed possibilities. The focus on participation in institutions of child-centred development will suffer from such fundamental inequities underlying the life of children in society. A development concept, such as the Child-Centred Community Development of Plan International, which aims at the development of the child through progress in the local community, with a focus on the poor households, in the end has a higher potential of providing rights to the child and their families.

A problem with the welfare approach, and with the participation approach, has always been that it depoliticises the solutions. Children are granted some benefits that they otherwise (without charitable intervention) would have to forego, but the approach never questions the environment, which causes the marginalisation of the children and their communities in the first place. The conditions in which children are living, the opportunities they seem to have and the problems, impediments, and dangers they encounter in their daily lives, suggest that there is a need for a policy based on the three P's: Participation, Protection, and Provision.

The relevance of the three P's approach, even if difficult to define unambiguously, is obvious. Provision will bring resources and support to children in poor families, in poor areas, and in poor countries and help them to work themselves out of conditions of deprivation, misery, and vulnerability. Protection will help them to live a life free of physical violence and intimidation and to be shielded from social and economic turbulence. Participation will allow them to enter the public space as respected individuals who can grow into social beings with self-esteem and agency.

The three P's, however, are not free goods. Interventions are likely to be decided upon in terms of priorities and efficiencies. Although progress (or in other words, sustainable development that benefits society at large) may not be within the means of child-centred development aid organisations, locally some efforts could be undertaken to improve the economic position of marginalised families. Protection, Provision and Participation then remain as the three P's of child-centred strategies. Decisions in favour of prioritising one of them over the other are to be based on knowledge of the socioeconomic reality in the target area. In the rural areas of Burkina Faso, Tanzania, and India, for example, the obvious need is for infrastructural provisions which will allow children to attend schools and health centres. Unless provisions are brought to the local environment, the children in the poor families (the majority of the children) will continue to live a marginalised existence, and will not acquire those capacities that will allow them to participate as citizens in mainstream society.

Throughout the study, the absence or presence of provisions has been felt. Provision is a responsibility of the state and of the adult world. Childhood is constructed through such provisions. Whenever the state had provided good schools in the neighbourhood, children did not have to fight for their right to have a school. The study, particularly the Indian example of Rajasthan, has shown that, for example, proper provisions of locally embedded schools are extremely beneficial for children, boys and girls alike, in poor neighbourhoods. Children should be able to participate in the childhood institutions, particularly the educational system, long before participation as agents of change would become feasible. Within the space earmarked to them and run for them by adults, the school for example, getting children involved in setting up sports meetings, cultural events, charity initiatives, and environmental projects (examples of which we found in Nicaragua, India, and Vietnam) will be the next possible step in participation. It allows the children to develop their talents and to put their idealism into practice. The active involvement of children in Vietnam in cleaning operations and in looking after poor households, although initiated by adults, probably have a much higher potential of instilling in the child the sense of responsibility and social awareness which UNICEF referred to in the quote above on authentic child participation. Such activities respond to the interests of the child; they involve children socially and develop their sense of self-esteem.

Understanding the importance of involving children in the making of the world around them is one thing, but the translation of this understanding into a realistic involvement in community development is another. A social transformation that is, ideally, guided by children and by the interests of the children is a tall claim, but we have come across sufficient cases and instances to suggest that there is an important lesson to be learned from involving children. A child obviously has to be actually involved in his/her own development. That is the way forward. It is important to ensure that participation remains real, and that it does not become a token formality. For instance, consulting with children so that they can determine the colour of the furniture in their schools is a step in the right direction, because it involves the children in shaping their environment. On the other hand, the exercises in which children express their own priorities for development, or how an ideal school building should look like, are a sound antidote to adult-inspired programmes and it is worthwhile to listen to them.

We have noticed that the wishes of adults and children were often similar—roads, school, hospitals, income—but that the children had separate wishes which were all related to their own life experience: good and trustworthy teachers, easy access to water, cleanliness, more respect from adults. Unfortunately, they were usually not listened to. Adultism was very much present in all the research areas. Children did not always have their own space and spent much of their time with the adults, sitting around and listening in on their conversations. This helped them to be knowledgeable about the world, but on the other hand, adults were not in the habit of asking children for their opinions, their thoughts, their worries, their problems, or their desires.

The attitude underlying the adult–child relationship is based on hierarchy, stemming from a traditional society. In Vietnam for example, there is a division between two types of people: *sö* and *sù*. *Sö* are grandfather, father, husband, and elder brothers. These people are responsible for managing and controlling the family and educating others. *Sù* (children, wife, younger brothers and sisters) are under the control and educated by *sö*. It is the negation of agency. Women and children belonging to *sù* did do not have the right to make decisions for their own family or for themselves. In contemporary society, many important changes have taken place and children and women's rights are more and more respected. However, the remnants of the traditional cultural patterns still persist within the family and in social patterns and norms, especially in rural and mountainous areas. This is even more the case in countries such as Nicaragua, where machismo is still very much alive, and affects all relations between males and females and between adults and children.

The study in Vietnam concluded that children now have a voice in society and in law; the family, the school, and the community are increasingly respecting their voices. Appealing to public opinion at large and changing awareness about children within the communities is very important in building a better society for children. Vietnam could be taken as an example of how to do it. The media have played an active role in propagating the messages, and the UN Child Rights Convention has been translated into Vietnamese and some other ethnic languages. More than six million Vietnamese children have studied the convention and Vietnamese law. This could be taken as a good example for implementation in other countries, where the knowledge of the new culture of child rights is less familiar.

Many children we spoke with described the society they live in as one in which they are embedded in and looked after but also as a society which sometimes frightened them for its crime, harassment, rape, hunger, corporal punishment, and diseases. They spoke of how they have to find solutions if parents or family members cannot provide them with food, money, or school materials; and they explained how they sometimes have to drop out of school or get sexual relationships in exchange for these. But despite these sorrows and fears, most children showed hope and motivation for change. They had hopes for the future and used metaphors for that future: becoming a doctor, a teacher, or a nurse. The self-esteem observed in this study was outstanding. Most children and adolescents whom we interviewed had a positive self-image, apparent by how they consider themselves important, capable, and loved by their families. A good future, the children explained, depends on having a family, studies, good behaviour, and the avoidance of drug addiction and involvement in criminal activities. Both a positive self-image and positive expectations for the future are elements that can empower the development of children and adolescents.

But the same children sometimes felt as if they could not influence or affect certain situations. Some examples of situations on which children felt they had only little, if any, impact are: poverty, geographic isolation, the limited access to resources. Children are affected by these issues in different degrees, depending on the income and status of their parents, whether they went to school or not, the amount of time and energy spent working, the age and gender of the child, the level of education, and the rural/urban divide. Poverty and access to resources are more acute in rural areas and more children in rural areas spend a considerable amount of time and energy on household jobs and on money-generating activities. Such differences were found between the children in rural Mwanza and the children in urban Dar es Salaam, in the highlands of Vietnam and Hanoi, in the villages of Bihar and New Delhi, in the Sahel villages and in Batie, etc.

It is important to listen to children so that they can voice their needs and their capacities, but it remains important that adults assess the strategies that children may like to use from the standpoint of a universal concept of child rights. Some strategies employed by children, like calling in sick, avoiding the difficult choices and hard work (in school and at home), joining a gang, using alcohol and drugs to forget, are strategies which reveal agency, but improper agency. The children themselves feel that most of the negative forms of child labour result from poverty and from conditions that they are incapable of changing. Therefore their agency, in effect, is a 'second class' kind of agency, directed towards short-term solutions, often with undesirable consequences.

Agency, in short, should be based on an active development by the child, a careful listening by the adults to all possible signals and at the same time, a proactive institutional intervention by the adult world, without relinquishing responsibility, directed at changing cultural and economic structures that impose severe constraints on a child-centred development of all children, poor and rich, female and male.

The careful listening, finally, tells us that children are constrained in their structure and that any intervention needs to work on the surrounding structure. The focus in recent years on the individualised child and tapping its agency to the brim has tended to isolate policies from the highly iniquitous structure in which so many millions of children in the developing world are constrained to live. The Convention on the Rights of Children deals with Participation, Protection, and Provision. Participation is multi-interpretable and may not have a policy priority under most circumstances. Protection and Provision, for which the responsibility will remain predominantly with the state and supported by NGOs, is what children throughout this book have told us as a universal demand: access to education, good health services, and no need for child labour.

Bibliography

Ariès, Phillippe. 1964. *L'Enfant et La Vie Familiale Sous l'Ancien Régime*. Paris: Éditions du Seuil (1973. *Centuries of Childhood*. Harmondsworth: Penguin).

Basu, Kaushik, and P.H. Van. 1998. 'The Economics of Child Labor'. *American Economic Review* 88:412–427.

Black, Maggie. 2004. *Opening Minds, Opening Up Opportunities: Children's Participation in Action for Working Children*. London: Save the Children.

Boyden, Jo. 1997. Childhood and the Policy Makers: A Comparative Perspective on the Globalization of Childhood. In *Constructing and Deconstructing Childhood: Contemporary Issues in the Sociological Study of Childhood*, ed. A. James and A. Prout. London: The Falmer Press.

Boyden, Jo, B. Ling, and W. Myers. 1998. *What Works for Working Children*. Florence: UNICEF and Radda Barnen Sweden.

Chambers, Robert. 1983. *Rural Development: Putting the Last First*. Harlow: Longman.

Chinh, Nguyen Van. 2000. Work Without a Name: Changing Patterns of Child Work in a Northern Vietnamese Village. Dissertation, Amsterdam.

Corsaro, William. 1997. *The Sociology of Childhood*. Thousand Oaks, California: Pine Forge Press.

Cussianovich, Alejandro. 2002. Approaches to a Human Rights Related Typology of Child Labour. Conference Paper in *German NGO Forum on Child Labour*, 22–24. Hattingen.

ENDESA. 2001. *Indicadores Sociales de la Ninez Nicaraguense*. Managua: Enquestra de Demografia y Salud.

FEB. 2001. *Political Handbook and NGO Calendar 2002*. Dar es Salaam, Tanzania: Friedrich Ebert Stiftung.

Feeny, Thomas, and Jo Boyden. 2004. Acting in Adversity—Rethinking the Causes, Experiences and Effects of Child Poverty in Contemporary Literature. QEH Working Paper Series QEHWPS 116, Oxford.

Fernando, Jude. 2001. 'Children's Rights: Beyond the Impasse'. *Annals of the American Academy of Political and Social Science* 575 (May): 8–24.

Frones, Ivar. 2005. Structuration of Childhood: An Essay on the Structuring of Childhood and Anticipatory Socialization. In *Studies in Modern Childhood: Society, Agency, Culture*, 267–282. Basingstoke: Palmgrave MacMillan.

Goetze, Anne Marie. 1994. 'Alternative System of Enquiry for a Sustainable Agriculture'. *IDS Bulletin* 2, no. 2.

Govinda, R., ed. 2002. *India Education Report: A Profile of Basic Education*. New Delhi: Oxford University Press.

Grossman, Benjamin. 2000. *El Empleo en Instituto Primsma: Las Politicas Sobre la Pobreza en Bolivia*. La Paz: Plural Editores.

Hart, Roger. 1992. Children's Participation: From Tokenism to Citizenship. In *Innocenti Essay No. 4.* Florence: UNICEF ICDC.
———. 1997. *Children's Participation.* New York: UNICEF.
ICDS. 1976. *Education in Vietnam: Trends and Differentials.* Hanoi: Inter-Censal Demographic Survey, Statistical Publishing House.
INE. 2001. *Indicadores Sociales y Economica.* La Paz: Instituto Nacional de Estadistica.
INSD. 1999. *Profil et Evolution de la Pou vreté au Burkina Faso. Onagadougou: Ministere de l'Econonomie.* (http://www.insd.bf/.)
IPEC. 2002. *Tanzania: Child Labour in the Informal Sector; A Rapid Assessment.* Geneva: ILO.
James, Allison, Chris Jenks, and Alan Prout. 1998. *Theorising Childhood.* Cambridge: Polity Press.
James, A., and A. Prout, eds. 1997. *Constructing and Reconstructing Childhood: Contemporary Issues in the Sociological Study of Childhood.* London: The Falmer Press.
Johnson, Victoria, Edda Ivan-Smith, Gill Gordon et al. 1998. *Stepping Forward: Children and Young People's Participation in the Development Process.* Southampton: Intermediate Technologies Publications.
Katz, Cindy. 2004. *Growing Up Local: Economic Restructuring and Children's Everyday Lives.* Minneapolis: University of Minnesota Press.
Kuleana. 1999. *The State of Education in Tanzania, Crisis and Opportunity.* Mwanza: Centre for Children's Rights.
Kundu, Amitabh. 2006. *India, Social Development Report.* New Delhi: Oxford University Press.
Laderchi, Caterina Ruggeri. 2001. Participatory Methods in the Analysis of Poverty: A Critical Review. QEH Working Papers Number 62, Oxford.
Lansdown, Gerison. 2005. *Benchmarking Progress in Adopting and Implementing Child Rights Programming.* London: Save the Children Fund.
Le Thi Quy. 2003. Children and Development in Vietnam. In *Children and Agency, Report No. 7.* Amsterdam: IREWOC.
Liebel, Manfred. 2004. *A Will of Their Own: Cross-cultural Perspectives on Working Children.* London/New York: ZED.
Liebel, Manfred, Bernd Overwien, and Albert Recknagel. 2001. *Working Children's Protagonism.* Frankfurt: IKO.
Lieten, G.K. 2001. Child Labour: Questions on Magnitude. In *Child Labour: Policy Options,* ed. G.K. Lieten and B. White, 49–66. Amsterdam: Aksant Academic Publisher.
———. 2002a. 'Child Labour and Poverty: The Poverty of Analysis'. *Indian Journal of Labour Economics,* 2002, no. 3:451–464.
———. 2002b. 'Child Labour in India: Disentangling Essence and Solution'. *Economic and Political Weekly* 28 (December).
———. 2004. Child Labour in South Asia: An Account of Numbers. In *Small Hands in South Asia,* ed. G.K. Lieten, Ravi Srivastava, and S. Thorat, 37–60. New Delhi: Manohar.
———. 2005. 'Child Labour and Work: Numbers, From the General to the Specific'. *Indian Journal of Labour Economics,* no. 2.
———, A. Karan, and A. Satpathy. 2005. *Children, School and Work: Glimpses from India.* New Delhi: IHD/Amsterdam: IREWOC.
———, and B. White. 2001. *Child Labour: Policy Options.* Amsterdam: Aksant.
LLamos, David Layme. 2001. *Ninos Escolares Trabajadores en la Ciudad de El Alta.* La Paz: IDIS, Universidad Mayor de San Andres.
———. 2002. *Ninos Escolares Trabajadores en la Ciudad de Cochabamba y en el Municipio Rural de Tarata.* La Paz: IDIS, Universidad Mayor de San Andres.

————, and Antonio Moreno Valdavia. 2003. Ninos Estudiantes Trabojadores en Bolivia: Sector Urbano-Rural. In *Children and Agency, Report No. 8*. Amsterdam: IREWOC.

Miljeteig, Per. 2000. Creating Partnerships with Working Children and Youth. In *The World Bank: Social Projection Discussion Paper Series, No 0021*. Washington D.C.

Moreno, Antonio. 2001. *Ninos Escolares Trabajadores en la Municipio Rural de Chirapaca*. La Paz: IDIS, Universidad Mayor de San Andres.

————. 2002. *Niños Escolares Trabajadores de la Cuidad de Cruz y en el Municipio Rural de El Torno*. La Paz: Institutio de Investigaciones Sociológicas de la Universidad Mayor de San Andrés.

Myers, William. 1999. "Considering Child Labour: Changing Terms, Issues and Actors at the International Level'. *Childhood* 6, no. 1:13–26.

NBS. 2001. *Household Budget Survey 2000–2001*. Dar es Salaam: National Bureau of Statistics.

Nieuwenhuys, Olga. 1998. 'Global Childhood and the Politics of Contempt'. *Alternatives* 23, no. 3.

Nimbona, Godefroid, and G.K. Lieten. 2007. *Child Labour Unions: AEJT Senegal*. Amsterdam: IREWOC Foundation.

O'Malley, Kate. 2004. *Children and Young People Participating in PRSP Processes: Lessons from the Save the Children's Experiences*. London: Save the Children.

Omer, M. Omer. 2002. Burkina Faso. In *Children as Agents in Development, Report No. 4*. Amsterdam: IREWOC.

Oostra, Menno, and Leonor Malaver. 2003. *Bolivia: Mensen—Politiek - Economie- Cultuur - Milieu*. Amsterdam: KIT Publishers.

Postman, Neil. 1984. *The Disappearance of Childhood*. New York: Vintage Books.

Purdy, Laura. 1992. *In Their Best Interest? The Case Against Rights for Children*. Ithaca: Cornell University Press.

Qvortrup, Jens, ed. 1994. *Childhood Matters: Social Theory, Practice and Politics*. Aldershot: Avebury.

————. 2005a. Varieties of Childhood. In *Studies in Modern Childhood: Society, Agency, Culture*, ed. Jens Qvortrup, 1–20. Basingstoke: Palmgrave MacMillan.

————, ed. 2005b. *Studies in Modern Childhood: Society, Agency, Culture*. Basingstoke: Palmgrave MacMillan.

Reeuwijk, Miranda van. 2004. An Anthropological and Sociological Research about the Role of Children in Development, Tanzania. In *Children as Agents in Development, Report No. 10*. Amsterdam: IREWOC.

Rizzini, Irene, and Andrew Dawes. 2001. 'On Cultural Diversity and Childhood Adversity'. *Childhood,* 2001, no. 3:319.

Roschanski, Heike. 2007. *Working Children's Organisations in India*. Amsterdam: IREWOC Foundation.

Save the Children. 1997. *From Housework to Goldmining: Child Labour in Rural Vietnam*. Hanoi: Save the Children Vietnam.

Save the Children Alliance. *Child Rights Gender Index: Gender Equity Policy*. London/Stockholm: Save the Children Sweden.

Serra, Luis, and Marcia Castillo. 2003. *Situacion de la Ninez y Perspectivas de Desarollo Humano en Nicaragua*. Managua: Universidad de MesoAmerica.

Stephen, S., ed. 1995. *Children and the Politics of Culture*. Princeton: Princeton University Press.

Swift, A. 1998. *Working Children Get Organised*. London: International Save the Children Alliance.

UNAIDS. 2002. Epidemiological Fact Sheet on HIV/AIDS and Sexually Transmitted Infections. Dar es Salaam: USAIDS/UNICEF/WHO.

UNDP. 2002. *Informe de Desarrollo Humano en Bolivia*. La Paz, Bolivia: UNDP.

———. 2007. *Human Development Report 2007/2008*. New York: Palmgrave Macmillan.

UNICEF. 2000. The *State of the World's Children 2000*. Oxford: Oxford University Press.

———. 2002. *Proposal on African Girls Education Initiatives 2001–2003*. Dar es Salaam: Ministry of Education and UNICEF.

———. 2003. *The State of the World's Children*. Oxford: Oxford University Press.

———Vietnam. 2000. *Vietnam Children and Women: A Situation Analysis*. Hanoi: UNICEF.

Van den Berge, Marten. 2007a. *Working Children's Organisations in Peru*. Amsterdam: IREWOC Foundation.

———. 2007b. *Working Children's Organisations in Bolivia*. Amsterdam: IREWOC Foundation.

Vandenbroeck, Michel, and Maria Bouverne-De Bie. 2006. 'Children's Agency and Educational Norms: A Tensed Negotiation'. *Childhood* 13, no. 1:127–143.

White, Ben. 1999. 'Defining the Intolerable: Child Work, Global Standards and Cultural Relativism'. *Childhood* 6, no. 1:133–144.

Wolf, Eric. 1982. *Europe and the People Without History*. Berkeley: University of California Press.

Woll, Lisa. 2000. *The Convention on the Rights of the Child: Impact Study*. Stockholm: Save the Children.

World Bank. 1996. *The World Bank Participation Source Book*. http://www.worldbank.org/wbi/sourcebook/sbhome.htm.

Zelizer, Viviana. 1985. *Pricing the Priceless Child: The Changing Social Value of Children*. New York: Basic Books.

Author

G.K. (Kristoffel) Lieten (Belgium, 1946) studied in Antwerp, The Hague, Reading, and New Delhi, where he obtained degrees in linguistics, political science, and history respectively. He has worked extensively on political developments in South Asia and on issues related to development sociology. Lieten has been on the teaching staff at Department of Anthropology and Non-Western Sociology at the University of Amsterdam and presently holds the chair of Child Labour studies at the University of Amsterdam and at the International Institute of Social History in Amsterdam. He is the director of the IREWOC Foundation (Institute for Research on Working Children) and in that capacity Dr. Lieten has initiated several research projects on child labour and child agency in various countries across the globe. His recent books include: *Child Labour: Policy Perspectives* (2001, with Ben White); *Working Children around the World: Child Rights and Child Reality* (2004); *Children, Work and Labour: Glimpses from India* (2005); *Unequal Partners: Power Relations, Devolution and Development in Uttar Pradesh* (2002, with Ravi Srivastava); *Power, Politics and Rural Development* (2003); and *Views on Development: The Local and the Global in India and Pakistan* (2004).

Index